YORK NOTES

The Rape of the Lock & Selected Poems

Alexander Pope

Note by Robin Sowerby

 Longman

 York Press

YORK PRESS
322 Old Brompton Road, London SW5 9JH

PEARSON EDUCATION LIMITED
Edinburgh Gate, Harlow,
Essex CM20 2JE, United Kingdom
Associated companies, branches and representatives throughout the world

First published 2000
Second impression 2007

ISBN: 978-0-582-42453-1

Designed by Vicki Pacey
Phototypeset by Gem Graphics, Trenance, Mawgan Porth, Cornwall
Colour reproduction and film output by Spectrum Colour
Produced by Pearson Education Asia Limited, Hong Kong

CONTENTS

PART ONE

INTRODUCTION

HOW TO STUDY A POEM

Studying on your own requires self-discipline and a carefully thought-out work plan in order to be effective.

- First, learn to hear it: say it aloud, silently, whenever you read it. The poem lives in its sounds; poetry is as close to music and dance as it is to prose.
- A poem is not reducible to what you can extract from it at the end of the process of interpretation; it is a dramatic event, a *sequence* of thoughts and emotions.
- The only true summary of the poem is the poem. What can be summarised is one's experience of the poem, the process by which one arrives at a reading.
- What is the poem's tone of voice? Who is speaking?
- Does the poem have an argument? Is it descriptive?
- Is there anything special about the poem's language? Which words stand out? Why?
- What elements are repeated? Consider alliteration, assonance, rhyme, rhythm, **metaphor**.
- What might the poem's images suggest or symbolise? Do they fit together thematically?
- Is there a regular pattern of lines? Are they **end-stopped** (where the grammatical units coincide with line endings) or does the phrasing 'run over'?
- Can you compare and contrast the poem with other work by the same poet?
- Finally, every argument you make about the poem must be backed up with details and quotations. Always express your ideas in your own words.

This York Note offers an introduction to the poetry of Pope and cannot substitute for close reading of the text and the study of secondary sources.

Alexander Pope (1688–1744) was, without serious rival, the leading poet of his age and together with John Dryden (1631–1700) one of the two greatest poets of what has sometimes been called the **Neoclassical** period, that phase of English literature that extends from 1660 to about 1780. The word Neoclassical is a forbidding term that will not win him many friends these days, but the reputation of Pope's poetry, although it has had its ups and downs, stands secure. Nor is he a poet in reputation only, for even after the reaction against Neoclassical literature, his poetry has always actually been read. Through the vicissitudes of time and taste, *The Rape of the Lock* has continued to give pleasure and has been acknowledged to be the best of its particular kind in the whole of English literature.

In this celebrated **mock heroic**, the reader is transported into a world of delicate beauty and charm presided over by a group of delightful supernatural deities; the familiar social reality in which the poem is rooted undergoes a magical transformation through the comic use of the epic parallel so that what is newly created is a unique blend of fantasy and reality. Folly is mocked but in the most genial, good-humoured and good-natured way. Although Pope's **wit** delights in the imaginative world he creates for its own sake, he is also making a moral point. The poem perfectly fulfils what is regarded as the highest function of literature in the Renaissance tradition, equally to delight and to instruct.

The poem perfectly embodies, too, qualities that are peculiarly associated with the cultural achievements of its time. Its elegance, harmony, polish, refinement and panache evoke the values of the eighteenth century, values apparent equally in social living as in the artistic and cultural achievements of the age. Pope makes an amusing comedy of elegant social manners in his *Epistle to Miss Blount on her Leaving the Town after the Coronation* where he gallantly sympathises with an elegant young belle languishing in boredom far away from the pleasurable refinements of city living in the unsophisticated world of the country. Elegance, however, is never enough as we can see in the moral of *The Rape of the Lock* and in the moral concern manifested throughout his literary career.

Although in his **satire** he is the age's severest critic, Pope is **paradoxically** the great poetic representative of eighteenth-century urbanity and wit. This urbanity, a mental and moral product, as the word suggests, of living in the city, locates him as a poet of civilised life, defining its positives by exposing its negatives. There have been few poets who have brought a more concentrated ethical concern to bear upon the civilisation of their times. This is the context of his satire which manifests itself principally in two spheres: the social as in poems like the *Epistle to a Lady* and the literary in poems like *An Essay on Criticism, An Epistle to Dr Arbuthnot* and *The Dunciad*.

With the exception of *The Dunciad*, all these poems together with the Horatian **Imitations** are written in a form which Pope made his own and in which no other poet has excelled to the same extent: the ethical epistle or **moral essay**.

Although the upper-class society to which he addressed his epistles has long since passed away and may not be one for which a modern reader feels a natural sympathy, Pope has a broad view of human life (set out in *An Essay on Man*) within which his social and literary observation and criticism function, so that it is always possible to see beyond the eighteenth-century exterior of detail and example to types and issues that have a continued relevance in any kind of social or cultural world. For example, in the famous portrait of Sporus in *An Epistle to Dr Arbuthnot*, Pope exposes through satire an effete, toadying, unprincipled courtier of no moral or intellectual stability whose influence near the throne has sinister consequences. Though false courtiers may not be a social evil of much consequence today, it is not difficult to translate the character into types with which we are familiar in our society, those hangers-on in kitchen cabinets of prime ministers, for example. Similarly his image of the false critic in Atticus has continuing relevance. Writing in the next century Lord Byron said of him: 'He is the moral poet of all civilisation' by which he meant in part that his moral insights are such as do not date or become obsolete with the passage of time. Moreover, these insights are delivered with clear authority and emphatic force. Whether or not readers find themselves in sympathy with his moral positions, nobody can doubt that his poetry offers a vigorous moral challenge.

Pope is one of a small band of truly effective satirists in English. Of the kind in which he excels, trenchant belittling satire in verse, he is almost without rival. Those who like their satire to bite will enjoy the later poetry of Pope, whether in the formal verse epistles or in the epic satire of *The Dunciad*, whose serio-comic vision of Dullness emanating from Grub Street (an actual place in Pope's London) to cover the land and 'blot out order and extinguish light' has become part of general consciousness.

A poet's appeal will be as much in the ways things are said as in what is actually said, insofar as any hard and fast distinction is possible between content and form. Pope is one of the great masters of the English language. His expression, moulded into harmonious couplets, is always clear, forceful and sharp; it is also imaginative and suggestive. Pope wrote in an age when the shorthand term both for imaginative literature and its author was *wit*, a word originally meaning 'sense', 'understanding' or 'intelligence'; his poetry has a strong intellectual appeal. It shares this not only with its period but with the Renaissance generally where poetry (in sonnets, for example) has a stronger argumentative structure than has often been the case since. The idea that poetry is some kind of personal emotional unburdening, 'the spontaneous overflow of powerful feeling', in the famous formulation of Wordsworth, would have seemed limiting and faintly ridiculous to any of his fellow poets before him. Nor is it the case that the author of *Eloisa to Abelard* is incapable of moving the passions which are darkly evident too in the satires.

His mastery of language includes a mastery of poetic form, the closed **heroic couplet**, and of the **rhetorical** patterning that the couplet encouraged. He refined the heroic couplet, by which is meant but only that he made it more harmonious in its sound and arrangement but that, in cutting out various liberties and insisting on a severe regularity, he also made it in his own hands and those of other expert practitioners an instrument capable of more concentrated energy of expression. The refinement he wrought in the heroic couplet had a disciplined aim: the rigorous dismissal of any kind of superfluity on the principle that: 'Words are like leaves; and where they most abound, / Much fruit of sense beneath is rarely found.' (*An Essay on Criticism*, lines 309–10). Refinement of form in relation to Pope's handling of the heroic couplet is a misleading formulation if it suggests merely a superficial polishing up.

Pope's verbal artistry and witty way with words are second to none. In the struggle to put the best words in the best places, he seldom slips up:

> You think 'tis nature and a knack to please:
> 'But ease in writing flows from art, not chance;
> As those move easiest who have learn'd to dance.'
> (*The Second Epistle of the Second Book of Horace*, lines 177–9)

Part of this art comes from a close scrutiny of the poetic tradition from which he judiciously culled the right words, *les mots justes*. Putting them in the best places involved a mastery of rhetoric, the art of effective writing achieved by means of figures of arrangement such as Pope's favourite rhetorical figure, the **antithesis**. Those who have felt the force of this verbal artistry in his poetry will not be easily satisfied elsewhere.

But all poets have their detractors; Pope was a controversial figure in the life of his times. From an early age, he knew his own talent and in his later satirical verse he revelled in the power it gave him in the close-knit literary and social world of upper-class London.

> Whoe'er offends, at some unlucky time
> Slides into verse, and hitches in a rhyme,
> Sacred to ridicule his whole life long,
> And the sad burden of some merry song.
> (*The First Satire of the Second Book of Horace Imitated*, lines 77–80)

His was not a humble spirit: 'Yes, I am proud; I must be proud to see / Men not afraid of God, afraid of me' (*Epilogue to the Satires: Dialogue II*, lines 208–9). His contemporaries seldom criticised the quality of his verse but his satire aroused fear and envy and even on occasions alarmed his friends. He always claimed that he was on the side of the angels and that he used his power responsibly and only against deserving targets. There have always been those who have argued that he was self-deceived in this claim and that his satire was often prompted by vanity and vindictiveness. This will always be a question to be debated about his later work.

PART TWO

COMMENTARIES

The standard modern edition of the complete poems of Pope is John Butt, ed., The Twickenham Edition of the Poems of Alexander Pope, *in ten volumes, Methuen, 1938–68, with index (volume XI edited by Maynard Mack, 1969). This is available in a single edition (except for the Homer translations) edited by John Butt, Methuen, 1963. All the poems which are annotated and commented upon in this volume are available in: Pat Rogers, ed.,* Alexander Pope; Selected Poetry, *Oxford World's Classics, Oxford University Press, 1998. The order of the poems used here, roughly but not wholly chronological, is the traditional one which follows the arrangement made by Pope himself when he edited his own works at the end of his life.*

DETAILED SUMMARIES

THE RAPE OF THE LOCK (1717)
AN HEROI-COMICAL POEM

> In the wake of the family acrimony that followed the jest of Lord Petre in cutting off a lock of Miss Arabella Fermor's hair, it was suggested to Pope by a friend of all concerned, John Caryll (see I, 3), that he should 'write a poem to make a jest of it, and laugh them together again'

The first edition in two cantos was published in 1712. Encouraged by favourable reaction, Pope published an expanded version in 1714 adding the divine machinery, the card battle, and the cave of spleen. In 1717 the speech of Clarissa was added to Canto V in response to criticism that the poem lacked a moral.

Not much happens in *The Rape of the Lock*. That is part of the point.

Canto I: Belinda gets out of bed just at noon. The sylphs are introduced and their relation to mortals described. Belinda puts on her make-up.

Canto II: She sails down the Thames to Hampton Court. The Baron is introduced. He has designs, as yet unformed, on Belinda. Ariel, chief of the sylphs, has forebodings of some unknown disaster and threatens punishment for any neglectful sylphs.

Canto III: The scene at Hampton Court is described. Belinda, the Baron and a third person play the game of ombre. Belinda wins. They take coffee. The Baron suddenly has the idea of cutting the lock. Clarissa provides him with the scissors. The deed is done. Belinda screams. The Baron is triumphant.

Canto IV: Umbriel, the dusky gnome, now the presiding spirit in place of Ariel, visits the Cave of Spleen to confirm Belinda as one of the goddess's devotees. Thalestris laments her loss of 'honour'. Belinda bids Sir Plume demand the restoration of the lock. The Baron refuses. Belinda laments the cruelty of her fate.

Canto V: Clarissa offers good advice (try good humour rather than hysterical threats) but is ignored. The battle of the beaux and belles ensues. The belles win but the lock is lost and found to have ascended into the heavenly sphere where it has become a constellation.

An heroi-comical poem [subtitle] a better description than the one more generally used now, '**mock heroic**', which might suggest that the poem is mainly designed to mock epic. But any mockery of epic motifs is not the main point; the poet is juxtaposing the seriousness of epic, with its battles in which matters of life and death are decided, against the triviality of the subject matter of the poem, a quarrel over the loss of a lock of hair, a loss that, in the scale of human suffering, is decidedly minor. The form, motifs and style of epic are designed to put a perspective upon the triviality by comically blowing it up to absurd proportions. The heroi-comical, therefore, exploits an incongruity between form and content, between subject matter and treatment. (See Critical Approaches, on Rhetorical Devices, and Extended Commentaries, Text 1)

'TO MRS ARABELLA FERMOR' [DEDICATION]
Rosicrucian 'a supposed society or order reputedly founded by one Christian Rosenkreuz in 1614, whose members were said to claim various forms of secret and magic knowledge, as the transmutation of metals, the prolongation of life, and power over the elements and elemental spirits.' (*OED*)

CANTO I   Belinda awakens. The sylphs are introduced

Belinda wakes up at midday. The sylphs are introduced as guardian spirits of the fair sex. Their chief, Ariel, describes their origin, their nature and their relation to mortals below. Belinda gets out of bed and puts on her make-up.

The poem begins like an epic with a proposition or statement of the subject and an address to the muse. The opening is quite serious, the first comic note occurring when 'sleepless lovers, just at twelve, awake' (line 16). The sleeplessness of the lovers is a conventional idea; waking up at midday is doubtless also common in the aristocratic world of the poem: the union of the two offers an **ironic** comment on both. In the sylphs 'The light militia of the lower sky' (line 42), the gods and goddesses of classical epic are delightfully miniaturised. By making them correspond to certain female types in their previous mortal existence, Pope integrates them into the social world and at the same time comments upon it.

In the make-up scene, the language at the opening stresses self-idolatry in 'the sacred rites of pride' (line 128) and there is a pointed arrangement in the line (138) in which Bibles are to be found in the indiscriminate clutter of the dressing table, but the passage has its own beauty, apparent when compared to its source (given below). Like an epic hero, Belinda is arming for battle (line 139); she is putting on her war-paint and it works. Just like the poet who is painting her, she too is dressing nature to advantage.

4 **Belinda** Arabella Fermor
7 **Say what strange motive** at the opening of the *Aeneid* (I, line 11) Virgil bids his muse say what are the causes of Juno's anger, then asks whether such rage can dwell in heavenly minds
   Goddess the muse traditionally addressed by the epic poet
13 **Sol** the sun
17 **the slipper knocked the ground** the usual way to summon a servant
18 **pressed watch** a repeater
23 **birth-night beau** a young man dressed in the finery worn at court to celebrate royal birthdays

44 **box ... ring** a box in the theatre. The Ring (also called the tour or circus) was a fashionable route to drive along in Hyde Park

45 **equipage** 'a carriage and horses with attendant footmen' (*OED*)

46 **chair** a sedan chair

55 **chariots** carriages were so called

56 **ombre** a fashionable card game; compare bridge today; see III, lines 27ff below. This couplet recalls Virgil's description of the classical underworld as translated by John Dryden (*Aeneis*, VI, lines 890–1): 'The love of horses which they had, alive, / And care of chariots, after death survive.'

59 **termagants** scolds

60 **salamander** a kind of lizard, once thought to be able to live in fire

73 **spark** an elegant fashionable young man

85 **garters, stars, and coronets** worn by the nobility

89 **bidden blush** achieved by means of rouge

94 **impertinence** a trifle

96 **treat** an entertainment of food and drink

101 **sword-knots** ribbons tied to the hilt of a sword

115 **Shock** refers to a breed of dog; a lap-dog

121 **And now, unveiled** compare one of the sources for this passage in Dryden's translation of part of the Roman poet Juvenal's sixth satire on the subject of women:

She duly, once a month, renews her face;

Meantime it lies in daub, and hid in grease:

Those are the husband's nights; she craves her due,

He takes fat kisses, and is stuck in glue.

But, to the loved adulterer when she steers,

Fresh from the bath, in brightness she appears:

For him the rich Arabia sweats her gum,

And precious oil from distant Indies come,

How haggardly so'er she looks at home

The eclipse then vanishes; and all her face

Is opened, and restored to every grace. (lines 593–603)

125 **glass** the mirror

137 **patches** black beauty spots worn on the face; **bibles** are incongruous items amidst this dressing-table litter

144 **keener lightnings** a sparkle in the eye induced by belladonna

148 **Betty** generic name for a maid

CANTO II   The Baron has as yet unformed designs upon Belinda

Belinda sails down the Thames to Hampton Court. The Baron is introduced as a lover who has designs, as yet unformed, upon Belinda. The sylphs are described as they flutter about Belinda on her barge. Ariel, fearful of some unknown disaster, addresses them, warns them to be vigilant and threatens punishment for any negligence

The tribute to Belinda's beauty continues in the description of her sailing down the Thames. The praise when she is likened to the sun and called 'the rival of his beams' (line 3) is extravagant and the language is grand but gallantry predominates over irony. The Baron's sacrifice to the heavenly powers is comically reminiscent of the sacrifices and prayers made before battle by epic heroes. The beautiful lines describing the progress of the boat on the water (lines 48–52) are a prelude to the exquisite delicacy of the description of the sylphs that follows (lines 55–68), a passage often cited to illustrate Pope's imaginative powers at their best. The airy, insubstantial, indefinite, evanescent beauty of the sylphs is made to reflect perfectly the transient charm of the world over which they preside. Ariel's set speech begins on a high note when he describes their grander cosmic tasks and turns to comedy when he descends to their 'humbler province' (line 91) attending to the minutiae of the female world. The variety of disasters ominously threatened is comic in itself but also contains some moral point. The moral and the spiritual, the physical and material, are all jumbled together and seem to have the same value, as if to suggest that in Belinda's world there is no proper moral hierarchy. When Ariel threatens neglectful sylphs with punishments, these are fittingly miniaturised, making use of items from the dressing table: vials, pins, washes, bodkins, gums, pomatums and alum styptics. The threatening omens and the threat to the sylphs cleverly build suspense as the poem moves towards the climactic action.

25 **springes** snares for catching small animals
29 **Baron** Robert, seventh Lord Petre (1690–1713)
35 **Phoebus** epithet of Apollo, the sun god

45 **granted half his prayer** an epic motif: compare Virgil in Dryden's translation: 'Apollo heard and granting half his prayer / Shuffled in winds the rest, and tossed in empty air.' (XI, lines 1195–6)

64 **glittering textures** gossamers formerly supposed to be the product of sunburnt dew, not spiders

84 **painted bow** rainbow

97 **wash** a medical or cosmetic lotion

100 **flounce** 'an ornamental appendage to the skirt of a lady's dress' (*OED*)
furbelow 'the pleated border of a petticoat or gown' (*OED*)

105 **Diana's law** Diana was the goddess of chastity

113 **drops** diamond earrings

119 **seven-fold fence** shields in epic are invariably sevenfold

128 **bodkin** needle or hairpin

129 **pomatums** ointments

131 **styptics** astringents which stop bleeding

132 **rivelled** shrivelled

133 **Ixion** punished by Zeus for making advances to his wife Hera by being fixed to an eternally revolving wheel in Tartarus

CANTO III   After a game of cards the Baron cuts off Belinda's lock of hair

The social scene at Hampton Court is set. Belinda, the Baron and a third person play a game of cards in which Belinda is the winner. They take coffee. As he drinks, the Baron gets the idea of cutting the lock. Clarissa provides him with a pair of scissors. He advances behind Belinda as she is bending over her coffee. The sylphs are unable to protect her, so the deed is done. She screams; the Baron is triumphant.

The opening five and a half lines describing Hampton Court are suitably grand until, with statesmen predicting the fall of domestic beauties, there is a descent into a world of social gossip. The Queen takes counsel and tea while her courtiers are variously engaged in 'instructive' talk. There is pointed humour in the juxtaposition of the grand and the trivial here as we hear what it is they are talking about. The social realism of the opening gives way to the excitement of the card game wittily conceived as an epic battle. Scholars confirm that the game is played realistically and according to the rules. The underlying realism is confirmed in the description of the playing cards themselves, even to the details of the orb held by the king of clubs and the head of the diamond king, the only one in profile. The epic parallel serves both to put a perspective upon the importance attached to card games in this social world of rather trivial pursuits and at the same time to bring out the intensity and real emotional passion with which human beings can become involved in play. That the Baron should conceive the idea of cutting the lock as they partake of the coffee, a stimulant, is another facet of the underlying psychological realism that involves us in the plot. His speech of triumph is a mock version of the triumphant speech allowed to heroes after they have killed their opponent in battle. At a climactic action in epic, the epic narrator often intervenes in his story directly to address his characters as does the poet here with his serio-comic disquisition on the power of steel.

1   **Close by those meads**   for discussion of the opening, see Critical Approaches, Rhetorical Devices in *The Rape of The Lock*

12   **visit**   a formal call

27   **ombre**   a game with three players and a pack of forty cards. The player taking the most tricks wins. Belinda wins the first four, and then the Baron the next four, so that the final trick decides the game

30   **sacred nine**   each player has nine cards

33   **matadore**   one of three cards of high value including the ace of spades and ace of clubs and one other ace depending upon what were trumps

42   **halberts**   a combination of spear and battle-axe

44   **velvet plain**   describing the green cloth-covered card table but reminiscent of the Trojan plain

46   **Let spades be trumps**   compare the divine fiat in Genesis 'Let there be light'

49   **Spadillio**   the ace of spades. Belinda, perhaps imprudently, plays her winning cards first

51   **Manillio**   the two of spades

53   **Basto**   the ace of clubs

61   **Pam**   the knave of clubs, which in the game of Lu (or Loo) was the chief trump

67   **Amazon**   doughty women warriors in Greek myth, here the queen of spades

92 **codille** the winner was said to have given codille to the loser

106 **berries** coffee berries, first roasted then ground

107 **shining altars of Japan** lacquered tables

110 **China's earth** porcelain cups

122 **Scylla** daughter of **Nisus**. His safety and that of his kingdom depended upon a lock of hair which Scylla stole to betray him to his enemy Minos with whom she had fallen in love. She was punished for her impiety by being turned into a bird

147 **forfex** scissors

165 **Atalantis** refers to a novel recently published in 1709 by Mary Manley notorious for its libels which had led to her arrest

167 **visits** made in the evening when the lady was escorted by servants bearing lights

CANTO IV The Cave of Spleen

Belinda is now enraged. Ariel, his power broken, withdraws from her and his place as presiding spirit is taken by Umbriel who visits the Cave of Spleen to ask the goddess Spleen to make Belinda one of her devotees. The goddess consents. Belinda's anger is fanned by Thalestris who vividly imagines how people will gossip about her. Belinda flies to Sir Plume and bids him demand that the Baron surrender the lock. The Baron refuses. A grief-stricken Belinda laments the cruelty of her fate.

> The gaiety and airiness of the opening cantos give way to something darker and more grotesque as Belinda's smiling beauty is disfigured by anger and vexation. Earlier, on the Thames and with Ariel in attendance, 'Belinda smiled, and all the world was gay' (II, line 52); now when she is touched with 'chagrin', 'That single act gives half the world the spleen' (line 78). The Cave of Spleen is a version of the classical underworld tailor-made for the small world of polite society. In Virgil's *Aeneid*, the hero journeys to the underworld and encounters there the stuff of nightmares, all the terrifying monsters of classical myth and a variety of horrors in allegorical form, like Famine, Disease and Poverty. In the cave, the allegorical monsters are Headaches and Affectation. The monstrous takes a form appropriate to the female world as jars sigh and 'a

goose-pie talks' (line 52). Pope's own note on this is instructive: 'Alludes to a real fact, a lady of distinction imagined herself in this condition'. Here is the potential for madness, as what is repressed in the polite and formal world of the *beau monde* rises to the surface. The long set speech of Thalestris is a powerful piece of **rhetoric**, comic in its reference, but seriously revealing the shallowness of the code of honour by which high society lives. The mood suddenly changes to the purely comic with the clipped utterances of the absurd Sir Plume. Belinda's lament, a mock version of the sort of speech in which a tragic figure recognises past error, ends with a comic couplet revealing that appearances are the be-all and end-all in this shallow world.

8 **manteau** a loose upper garment worn by women

13 **Umbriel** the Latin word *umbra* means shadow

16 **Cave of Spleen** compare Ovid's Cave of Envy in the *Metamorphoses*, II, lines 760ff. Spleen was a fashionable complaint of high society associated with melancholia and moroseness

18 **vapour** the spleen was also called the vapours, supposedly induced by a misty climate

20 **east** a wind favourable to spleen

24 **Megrim** headache

40–6 **phantoms ... spectres ... angels** hallucinations were symptoms of the spleen. Here Pope satirises scenic effects in contemporary opera and pantomime

51 **pipkin** a small earthenware boiler

Homer's tripod an allusion to *Iliad*, XVIII, lines 440–8 in Pope's version

56 **spleenwort** a kind of fern with medicinal properties supposed to cure the spleen, reminiscent here of the Golden Bough carried by Aeneas as his passport through Hades, the underworld of the dead in classical myth

62 **physic** medicine

64 **in a pet** in a fit of ill humour

69 **citron waters** brandy flavoured with citron or lemon rind

71 **airy horns** horns, a conventional image suggesting adultery; airy because they are imaginary here

82 **Ulysses** Homer's hero who in *Odyssey*, X, is given a bag enclosing the storm winds which his companions foolishly unleash with dire effects

109 **toast** a lady whose beauty was honoured with raised glasses in company

114 **Exposed through crystal** displayed under glass as in a finger ring

117 **Hyde Park Circus** see note on I, line 44

118 **Bow** St Mary le Bow is in Cheapside, the site of business and commerce and therefore no place for a person of fashion

124 **nice conduct** fine management

clouded cane a variegated walking-stick

133 **But by this lock** recalls the oath of Achilles, *Iliad*, I, lines 309–17 in Pope's version

Now by this sacred sceptre, hear me swear,
Which never more shall leaves or blossoms bear ...
This sceptre, formed by tempered steel to prove
An ensign of the delegates of Jove,
From whom the power of law and justice springs:
(Tremendous oath! Inviolate of kings)
By this I swear, when bleeding Greece again
Shall call Achilles, she shall call in vain.

156 **bohea** a blend of black tea

161 **omens** common in epic; omens foreshadow Dido's death in Virgil's *Aeneid*

164 **Poll** the pet parrot

CANTO V   The battle intensifies; the lock cannot be found

When the Baron is obdurate, Clarissa advises that good humour might prevail where anger and hysteria are failing. Her good advice is ignored; the battle intensifies. Belinda throws snuff at the Baron and threatens to spear him with a bodkin if he does not restore the lock. But the lock cannot be found. It transpires that it has been spirited up to heaven where it becomes a constellation.

See Extended Commentaries, Text 1, for discussion of lines 7–66. Clarissa gives good advice which is ignored. The battle of the beaux and belles ensues. The language in which the battle is described recalls epic but the weapons are frowning looks and cutting remarks until Belinda resorts to snuff and a bodkin. When Jove, king of the gods, weighs the men's wits against Belinda's hair in his scales, the hair outweighs the men's wits, so that superficially the comic conclusion deflates the men and gives the victory to Belinda. But, in epic, the sinking scale means death, which here signifies the loss of the hair and the fact that it will not be restored in the poem (or in life). Pope's **wit** gives this allusion like many of the others a double significance which perfectly foreshadows the outcome he has designed. The lock, having been lost in the confusion, is finally transfigured and becomes a constellation. In the final couplet, this lock will inscribe Belinda's name in the stars. 'This lock' is also the poem that will make (and has made) Belinda famous.

5 **the Trojan** Aeneas whom **Dido** begged not to leave her for Italy. When he left she committed suicide

6 **Anna** Dido's sister

9 **Say** in **parody** of Sarpedon's speech, see Extended Commentaries, Text 1

14 **side-box** in the theatre men sat in the side boxes, women in the front boxes

20 **smallpox** Lord Petre (the Baron) died of smallpox in 1713 after the first edition of the poem. This speech was added in 1717 to 'open the moral of the poem' (Pope)

24 **paint** put on make-up

40 **whalebones** to stiffen the petticoat

45–52 **So when bold Homer ... flash of day** Pope's *Iliad*, XX, lines 91ff. (see Extended Commentaries, Text 1); **Pallas** is another name for Athene; **Mars** is the god of war; **Latona** is the mother of Apollo; **Hermes** is the messenger of the gods; **Jove**'s weapon is the thunderbolt; **Neptune** is god of the sea and causes earthquakes; the **pale ghosts** inhabit Hades which is under the earth

53 **sconce** a pendant candlestick

60 **metaphor, and ... song** in mockery of the exaggerated language of love songs

62 **Dapperwit** character in Wycherley's *Love in a Wood, or St. James' Park* (1671)

63 **Sir Fopling** character in Etherege's *The Man of Mode, or Sir Fopling Flutter* (1676)

64 **'Those eyes ... so killing'** from an opera called *Camilla* performed in 1706

65 **Maeander** a winding river in Asia Minor

71 **golden scales** in parody of epic; see Dryden's *Aeneis*, XII. line 1054:

Jove set the beam; in either scale he lays
The champions' fate, and each exactly weighs.
On their side, life and lucky chance ascends;
Loaded with death, that other scale descends.

78 **on his foe to die** the verb die can refer to sexual orgasm; see IV, lines 54 and 175–6 for further bawdy innuendo

88 **bodkin** a hairpin or clasp; its history recalls in parody that of Agamemnon's sceptre; see Pope's *Iliad* II, lines 129–36:

> The golden sceptre, of celestial frame,
> By Vulcan formed, from Jove to Hermes came:
> To Pelops he the immortal gift resigned;
> The immortal gift great Pelops left behind,
> In Atreus' hand; which not with Atreus ends,
> To rich Thyestes next the prize descends;
> And now the mark of Agamemnon's reign,
> Subjects all Argos, and controls the main.

105 **Othello** the handkerchief is a crucial element in the plot; a serious example of dire effects springing from amorous causes

122 **tomes of casuistry** minutely reasoned philosophy

125 **Rome's great founder** Romulus who ascended to heaven during an eclipse. He then appeared to Proculus in a vision ordering the Romans to sacrifice to him as to a god

129 **Berenice's locks** the wife of Ptolemy III who pledged to make a votive offering of her hair if her husband returned victorious from war. The offering was subsequently stolen and thought to have been made into a constellation by Zeus

136 **Rosamonda's lake** a pond in St James's Park

137 **Partridge** the absurd John Partridge, a contemporary astrologer who repeatedly predicted the deaths of the Pope and the king of France (a rival kingdom) without success

138 **Galileo's eyes** the telescope

Eᴘɪsᴛʟᴇ ᴛᴏ ᴍɪss ʙʟᴏᴜɴᴛ, ᴏɴ ʜᴇʀ ʟᴇᴀᴠɪɴɢ ᴛʜᴇ ᴛᴏᴡɴ
ᴀꜰᴛᴇʀ ᴛʜᴇ ᴄᴏʀᴏɴᴀᴛɪᴏɴ (1717)

Zephalinda leaves fashionable London for the unsophisticated countryside

The coronation is that of George I in 1714. This poem is discussed in Extended Commentaries, Text 2.

---

4 **spark** a fashionable young man

7 **Zephalinda** a name used by Teresa Blount, suggesting youth and beauty from zephyr, a spring wind

11 **plain-work** simple sewing as opposed to intricate embroidery involving purling stitches

15 **bohea** a blend of black tea

24 **whisk ... sack** the entertainment and the drink of the less sophisticated

26 **buss** 'an enthusiastic kiss' (*OED*)

38 **flirt** literally means a sudden movement of the fan

47 **Gay** John Gay, who wrote *The Beggar's Opera*, a close friend of Pope

48 **chairs** sedan chairs

E LOISA TO ABELARD (1717)

> **Eloisa, now a nun, recalls her passionate love for Abelard, a monk, and the dreadful consequences of it**

The discovery of letters from Abelard causes Eloisa, now leading an austere religious life in a convent, to recall the love affair she had with her former tutor. She experiences a great outpouring of grief and regret (lines 41–58). She remembers the heaven of falling in love (lines 59–72). She praises the love they shared together as of a value above all others (lines 73–98). She recalls the horror of the crime that resulted in the castration of Abelard and her grief when she was removed to a convent still only able to think of her lover (lines 99–118). She beseeches Abelard to come to her, then she bids him make her soul quit Abelard for God (lines 119–28).

She prays that God will care for his flock but feels her prayers are to no avail amid her sadness (lines 129–51). Her thoughts turn to Abelard again. The surrounding landscape is no longer an aid to meditation but casts a gloom which finds a responding echo in her (lines 152–70). Here she must stay till death allows a reunion (lines 171–6). She prays for assistance but questions her own motives, for she does not repent of her love for Abelard. Yet she curses her innocence. She cannot forget him. She questions her feelings and bids Abelard help her to subdue nature in pursuit of God (lines 177–206).

She envies the lot of the vestal virgin whose consciousness is untainted and whose sleep secure; by contrast she feels guilt and dreams of Abelard, dreams that end in nightmare leaving her grief-stricken (lines 207–48). Abelard by contrast is free from such disturbance [as a result of his physical punishment]. She invokes him again (lines 248–62). His image comes between her and God and nullifies her religious life (lines 263–76). She bids him come to her as she prays and separate her from God, then abruptly dismisses him, trying to renounce him so that she can be in a state of grace (lines 277–302).

In her cell she imagines she hears a spirit calling her to eternal rest. She desires to follow, bids Abelard the 'last sad office pay' and catch her dying breath though as a religious figure (lines 303–36) – rather than as a lover. She prays that when he dies he will ascend to heaven in ecstasy and that they may be buried in one grave to be a warning example to other lovers: 'Oh may we never love as these have loved!' (lines 337–52). May some poet who is unhappy in love sing of our story to 'soothe my pensive ghost'.

> This poem is frequently cited to illustrate Pope's ability as a poet of the passions. In his own words it depicts a conflict between 'grace and nature, virtue and passion'. Nature and passion may be deemed the winners: Eloisa is unable to repent of, renounce or forget her passion for Abelard which makes a mockery of her religious life. At the end the epistle affirms the memory of their love and Eloisa hopes that Abelard will officiate at her death.
>
> The alternative life of the spirit that Eloisa is living in the convent is stern but the conflict in her is affecting because it is not represented as unduly harsh and repressive. Part of her does indeed wish wholeheartedly to embrace the God whom she nowhere blames or berates.
>
> The evocation of the convent and its surroundings is a memorable part of the epistle. The gloomy **Gothic** background (lines 1–3, 17–24, 141–4, 155–70, 303–8), unusual in poems of the period, mirrors the inner landscape of Eloisa's mind and does indeed become her imaginative landscape when she is cursed with the 'dear horrors of all-conscious night' (line 229) when 'Provoking demons all restraint remove / And stir within me every source of love' (lines 231–2).

ELOISA TO ABELARD continued

> Alas, no more! methinks we wandering go
> Through dreary wastes, and weep each other's woe,
> Where round some mouldering tower pale ivy creeps,
> And low-browed rocks hang nodding o'er the deeps. (lines 241–4)

Like the Gothic novels that were to come later in the eighteenth century, *Eloisa* delves below the surface of conscious life in its representation of repressed erotic impulses.

- 4 **Vestal** a virgin priestess of the Roman goddess Vesta, by transference, a nun
- 7 **Abelard** an historical figure, Pierre Abelard (1079–1142), a French theologian. Eloisa (Heloïse) was one of his pupils. She has just come upon a letter talking of their love written by Abelard to a third person
- 20 **horrid** bristling
- 64 **lambent** radiant
- 99 **sudden horrors** Eloisa is thinking of the castration of Abelard ordered by her father to end the affair
- 110 **bade the world farewell** in entering the monastery
- 133 **You raised these hallowed walls** Abelard founded the nunnery
- 177 **the spouse** the nun is regarded as the bride of Christ; see also line 219
- 212 **Obedient slumbers** taken from 'Of a religious house' by Richard Crashaw (*c*.1612–49)
- 220 **hymeneals** wedding songs
- 343 **May one kind grave** they were interred in adjoining monuments

E PISTLE TO A LADY (1735)

OF THE CHARACTERS OF WOMEN

> ### An attack on various types of women among Pope's own contemporaries

Pope summarised the argument of this poem in a headnote of his own:

'Of the characters of women (considered only as contra-distinguished from the other sex.) That these are yet more inconsistent and incomprehensible than those of men, of which instances are given even from such characters as are plainest, and most strongly marked; as in the affected, ver.7 etc. The soft-natured, [line]29. The cunning,

[line]45. The whimsical, [line]53. The wits and refiners, [line]87. The stupid and silly, [line]101. How contrarieties run through them all.

'But though the particular characters of this sex are more various than those of men, the general characteristic, as to the ruling passion, is more uniform and confined. In what that lies, and whence it proceeds, [line]207, etc. Men are best known in public life, women in private, [line]199. What are the aims, and the fate of the sex, both as to power and pleasure? [lines]219, 231.etc. Advice for their true interest, [line]249. The picture of an esteemable woman, made up of the best kind of contrarieties, [line]269 etc.'

> The poet makes adept use of the **metaphor** of painting first broached in line 5 and picked up in lines 15–20, 151–6, 181–92, 195–6. The metaphor is appropriate in a society where 'painting' meant making-up. Like the painter, the poet has to fix an essentially changeable subject in a particular attitude (lines 15–20), must not be too definite if he is to represent changeability which can only be suggested by 'some wandering touches, some reflected light' (line 153), and delights 'to draw the naked' (line 188), revealing the natural below the 'robe of quality' (line 189).

> The social world of *The Rape of the Lock* is here treated to a more scathing attack. The beauty of the scene in which Belinda makes up may be contrasted to the portrait of Sappho 'at her greasy task', likened in a belittling **simile** to 'morning insects, that in muck begun' (line 27). For comment on the veterans (line 243ff.) see Critical Approaches, on The Poet of Manners; see Extended Commentaries, Text 3, for comment on the portraits of Atossa and Cloe.

> The poet makes adept use of the 'frame'. The letter starts off in a conversational tone that suggests an intimate familiarity with the woman to whom it is addressed and implicates her in the satire by attributing to her the negative view of her sex with which he starts. At the end the addressee becomes the good example who can 'raise the thought and touch the heart' (line 250), is 'blest with temper' (line 257) and has 'sense and good humour' (line 292), thus disarming criticism that the poet is simply a misogynist. Yet, in the praise of the lady, the poet artfully continues the satire in a gentle

and **ironic** vein (lines 259–68) locating her firmly in the society of the female world he has just attacked.

7   **Arcadia's Countess** referring to *The Countesse of Pembrokes Arcadia* (1590) by Sir Philip Sidney. The countess was painted as a shepherdess by J. van der Vaart

8   **Pastora** a pastoral heroine as above

9   **Fannia** a Roman name possibly recalling a famous adulteress who saved the life of the Roman general Marius

10   **Leda** seduced by Zeus, king of the gods, in the form of a swan

12   **Magdalen** Mary Magdalene the repentant sinner

13   **Cecilia** patron saint of music

16   **romantic** extravagant

18   **trick her off** sketch her

20   **Cynthia** goddess of the moon, associated with change

21   **Rufa** redhead

22   **spark** a beau

23   **Locke** John Locke (1632–1704) the philosopher

24   **Sappho** the Greek poetess, referring to Lady Mary Wortley Montagu whose dirty clothes were often remarked upon

26   **mask** a masked ball, a masquerade

29   **Silia** the name suggests silence

31   **nice** punctilious. **Calista** is the penitent heroine of *The Fair Penitent* (1703) by Nicolas Rowe

32   **Simplicius** a commentator on the Stoic Epictetus

37   **Papillia** Latin for butterfly

43   **nice** discriminating

45   **Calypso** the nymph who detained Ulysses on his return from Troy

53   **Narcissa** the name suggests vanity

54   **wash** a lotion for the hair or the skin

57   **trim** dress

63   **Taylor** Jeremy Taylor, author of *Holy Living and Holy Dying* (1650–1), a popular devotional work

64   **citron** brandy flavoured with lemon peel

     Chartres a notorious rake

70   **punk** prostitute

71   **frank** free

78 **Tall-boy** handsome young lover in popular comedy

Charles popular name for a footman as is Betty for a maid and James for a coachman

79 **Helluo** Latin for glutton

80 **hautgout** anything with a strong accent

87 **Flavia** Roman name, probably an imaginary figure here

92 **Lucretia ... Rosamonda** two suicides

101 **Simo** a Roman name, perhaps chosen because it recalls the Latin word *simia* meaning an ape

110 **ratafie** cherry brandy

115 **Atossa** usually identified as the Duchess of Buckinghamshire (1682–1743), illegitimate daughter of James II. The name suggests whirlwind; see Extended Commentaries, Text 3

139–40 **bust ... temple** memorial monuments

155 **equal** unvaried or unshaded; Pope keeps up the painting metaphor

157 **Cloe** identified as Henrietta Howard, Countess of Suffolk (1681–1734); see Extended Commentaries, Text 3

182 **Queen** Caroline, wife of George II

184 **ball** the orb, symbol of power

193 **QUEENSBERRY** the Duchess of Queensberry was renowned for her beauty

198 **Mah'met** the name of the Turkish servant of George I

Parson Hale Stephen Hales, friend of Pope

207 **ruling passions** in the 'Epistle to Cobham. Of the Knowledge and Characters of Men', lines 174ff, Pope had given examples of the ruling passions of men

210 **sway** domination

239 **hags** witches; who hold annual meetings called **sabbaths**

240 **night** the time for formal visits

249 **friend** the addressee, Martha Blount

251 **ring** the fashionable driving circuit in Hyde Park

257 **temper** a good disposition, equanimity

266 **tickets** lottery tickets

codille see the note on *The Rape of the Lock*, III, line 92

267 **vapours** see *The Rape of the Lock*, IV, line 18

268 **China** both the kingdom and a vase or teacup

283 **Phoebus** Apollo, here as the god of prophecy

286 **simple prayer** presumably for beauty and riches

289 **The generous God** Phoebus, here as god of poetry and the sun by which gold generates in the earth

292 **good humour** compare *The Rape of the Lock*, V, line 30

An Epistle to Richard Boyle, Earl of Burlington (1731)
OF THE USE OF RICHES

The bad taste and waste of money exercised by those with wealth

Pope's own headnote gives a summary:

'The vanity of expense in people of wealth and quality. The abuse of the word taste, ver. [line]13. That the first principle and foundation in this, as it is in everything else, is good sense, ver. 39. The chief proof of it is to follow Nature, even in works of mere luxury and elegance. Instanced in architecture and gardening, where all must be adapted to the genius and use of the place, and the beauties not forced into it, but resulting from it, ver. 47. How men are disappointed in their most expensive undertakings for want of this true foundation, without which nothing can please long, if at all; and the rules will be but perverted into something burdensome or ridiculous, ver. 65, etc, to [line]98. A description of the false taste of magnificence; the first grand error of which is to imagine that greatness consists in the size and dimension, instead of the proportion and harmony of the whole, ver. 99; and the second, either in joining together parts incoherent, or too minutely resembling, or in the repetition of the same too frequently, ver. 105, etc. A word or two of the false taste in books, in music, in painting, even in preaching and prayer, and lastly in entertainments, ver. 133 etc. Yet Providence is justified in giving wealth to be squandered in this manner, since it is dispersed to the poor and laborious part of mankind ver. 169 … What are the proper objects of magnificence, and a proper field for the expense of great men, ver. 177, etc; and finally, the great and public works which become a prince, ver. 191 to the end.'

For Pope's aesthetic and his condemnation of rigid classicism, see Techniques, on Refinement of the Heroic Couplet. The earl is associated with a Palladian revival (examples of which are Chiswick House and Burlington House in London) and hailed at the end as a new Vitruvius. His example provides the frame for the satire of bad taste, most memorably ridiculed in Timon's Villa. All is for show. The library, however good it may look, contains no modern book. The villa and the life lived within it are the expression of 'civil pride' (line 166). Here is a vicious circle of bad taste, extravagance, bad judgement and poor moral sense. There is no question of art for art's sake in Pope's view. The artistic cannot be divorced from the moral. The vision at the end (line 177ff.) is of an artistic achievement that serves the nation and the public good.

7–10 **Topham, Pembroke, Hearne, Mead, Sloane** collectors. Hans Sloane's collection became the nucleus of the British Museum

13 **Virro** stemming from (Latin) *vir*: force, energy, vigour; here misdirected

15 **Sir Visto** a visto is a view seen at the end of an avenue of clipped trees, chosen doubtless to echo Virro. In neither case can any particular individual be identified

18 **Ripley** Thomas Ripley, architect and protégé of Robert Walpole, generally considered to be Britain's first prime minister

20 **Bubo** Bubb Doddington completed Eastbury in Dorset

25 **noble rules** Burlington had published Palladio's architectural designs in 1730

33 **pilaster** a square pillar projecting from a wall

34 **rustic** 'a surface artificially roughened or left rough-hewn' (*OED*)

36 **Venetian door** ' a door or window so called from being much practised at Venice by Palladio and others' (Pope). The door probably incorporated panes of glass, for Palladio exploited opportunities for light and airiness afforded by Mediterranean sun

38 **starve** used in the sense of starve for cold. Slavish imitators reproduce these features inappropriately in colder northern climes

39 **brother peer** Allen, Lord Bathurst, see line 178

44 **the seven** referring to the seven liberal arts that were the traditional university subjects: grammar, rhetoric, logic, geometry, arithmetic, astronomy and music

46 **Jones** Inigo Jones (1573–1652), famous English architect and designer who worked in the classical style

Le Nôtre André Le Nôtre (1613–1700) designer of the formal gardens at Versailles. Pope was an early champion of the informality that came to be associated with the great landscape gardeners of the eighteenth century. He put his ideas into practice in his own garden at Twickenham

57 **genius** guardian spirit

70 **Stowe** the house and gardens of Richard Temple, Viscount Cobham, in Buckinghamshire

72 **Nero's terraces** raised garden walks now in ruins in Rome

73 **parterres** level spaces in a garden 'occupied by an ornamental arrangement of flower beds of various shapes and sizes' (*OED*)

78 **Dr Clarke** a philosopher of unorthodox religious views whose bust, put there by Queen Caroline, was out of place in the hermitage in Richmond Park

80 **Quincunx** (replaced in the Oxford Classics edition by '**arbour**') originally five trees, one at the centre of a square formed by the rest

espaliers trellis-work for the support of trees, the trees so trained themselves

94 **dryads** (Greek myth) the spirits that inhabit trees

98 **alley** a walk in a garden generally bordered with trees or bushes; an avenue

99 **Timon** like Villario and Sabinus, an imaginary character, though many of the details were drawn from contemporary examples. Pope's enemies identified the villa with Cannons, the county seat of the Duke of Chandos, who had earlier been a patron of the poet. Pope denied this, and it is acknowledged to be a composite portrait

104 **Brobdignag** land of the giants in Swift's *Gulliver's Travels* (1726)

117 **Grove nods at grove** see Techniques, on Refinement of the Heroic Couplet

118 **platform** a raised terrace

123 **Amphitrite** a sea goddess

126 **Nilus' dusty urn** Nilus, the river god, whose urn is incongruously dry instead of being the source of a fountain

127 **majestic mien** a grand facial expression and demeanour

136 **Aldus ... du Suëil** Aldo Manutio (1449–1515), famous Venetian printer of the classics, and the Abbé du Suëil, an early eighteenth-century binder

138 **they are wood** refers to the practice of filling the upper shelves of libraries in great houses with painted wooden books

139 **Locke** John Locke (1632–1704), then recent philosopher of enlightened and tolerant views

146 **Verrio or Laguerre** Antonio Verrio (1639–1707)painted ceilings at Windsor and Hampton Court, and Louis Laguerre (1663–1721) at Blenheim

154 **Tritons** water outlets in the shape of the classical sea god, Triton

156 **hecatomb** a solemn sacrifice of a hundred beasts

160 **Sancho's dread doctor** in *Don Quixote* (1605) by Cervantes, the hungry Sancho is prevented from eating by a doctor who sends successive dishes away on the grounds that they are unhealthy, with the tap of his whalebone wand

162 **'God bless the King'** the toast at the end of the meal

176 **Ceres** Roman goddess of agriculture and fertility

194 **Vitruvius** Marcus Vitruvius Pollio, Augustan age author of the oldest and most influential treatise on architecture

204 **imperial works** a conscious echo of Dryden's translation of a famous passage in Virgil's *Aeneid* in which Rome's destiny is articulated: 'These are imperial arts, and worthy thee.' (VI, line 1177). In Virgil the imperial arts are the arts of government and the establishment of peace; in Pope it is the arts themselves which are to express and impress an imperial destiny of grandeur, refinement and beauty

A̲N EPISTLE TO DR ARBUTHNOT (1735)

Pope defends his 'modest satire' and rails against his critics

'This paper is a sort of bill of complaint', Pope wrote, 'begun many years since, and drawn up by snatches, as the several occasions offered. I had no thoughts of publishing it, till it pleased some persons of rank and fortune [Lord Hervey 'Sporus' (lines 305–33) and Lady Mary Wortley Montagu 'Sappho' (line 101)] to attack, in a very extraordinary manner, not only my writings (of which being public, the public may judge), but my person, morals, and family.' Lady Mary had written: 'Who but must laugh, this bully when he sees / A little insect shivering at a breeze.' In a note to the first edition, Pope wrote: 'This epistle contains an apology for the author and his writings.'

The poet complains that he is besieged by assorted scribblers and literary hacks; what has he done to deserve it? (lines 1–124). He reviews his literary career: 'Why did I write?' (line 125): 'But why then publish?' (line 135). Even in his early career when writing descriptive poetry he was attacked but he never replied (line 147). In early days he corrected himself if critics were right and simply smiled if they were wrong (lines 157–8). He gives his general opinion of most critics (lines 159–72). 'Were others angry?' If he replied he only gave people their due (lines 173–4). His 'modest satire' simply targeted the dull (lines 175–92). These are not worth bothering about but the talented Atticus is a more serious case of a man of letters who deserves a just rebuke as a false critic (lines 193–214). He may have become famous but never courted homage from the literary world (lines 215–230) leaving that to patrons like Bufo. He gives a portrait of Bufo, the self-important patron without true taste (lines 231–48). He comments more on the iniquity of patrons (lines 249–60). He prefers to be independent of patron and court (lines 261–70).

Why is he always being asked about his next work? (lines 271–82). He makes a declaration about his literary intentions (lines 283–304): 'A lash like mine no honest man shall dread, / But all such babbling blockheads in his stead' (lines 303–4). He attacks Sporus, the would-be wit and false courtier (lines 305–33). He continues to assert the integrity of his moral and poetic intentions; he has not and will not flatter or lie. He is proud that as a poet he did not wander long 'in fancy's maze' (line 340), in the self-indulgent world of the imagination, 'But stooped to truth and moralised his song' (line 341). He is a moralist in literature and in life not for fame but for the rightness of the cause, for 'virtue's better end' (line 342). And in this cause he has endured constant vilification and attack (lines 343–59). 'But why insult the poor, affront the great?' (line 360). Corruption is corruption wherever it is found (lines 361–7). In his life he has dealt charitably with those who have attacked him (lines 368–76).

He bids those who have attacked his family to hear what he has to say of his father and mother (lines 381–406). He pays a filial tribute to his father's simple goodness (lines 392–404). He prays for the continued life of his friend Arbuthnot and of his own aged mother (lines 407–end).

As the summary indicates, this epistle is a personal reply to various forms of attack that Pope endured in his literary career. It has the typical Popean blend of sharp satire against targeted enemies and **panegyric** of contrary examples, in this case his father and mother at the end and his own moral and poetical example throughout. Particularly marked is the intense condemnation of Sporus and the equally intense assertion of the poet's contrasting integrity that immediately follows. It is loosely constructed like the Roman satires of Pope's favoured satirical model, Horace, and is written in a familiar style (see Critical Approaches, on The Literary Critic & Standard-bearer of Cultural Values, and Satirical Ideal and Method). It contains two of Pope's most famous satirical portraits, those of Atticus and Sporus. For comment on Sporus see Critical Approaches, as above.

Atticus is a portrait of Joseph Addison, a *Spectator* editor and leading arbiter of taste. The portrait culminates in ridicule but before that there is nothing funny in the poet's dissection of the critic's pride that will not tolerate any rival to his position. The description of his critical and moral failings reveals something slightly sinister and contains one brilliant **paradox** 'Damn with faint praise' that has become part of general consciousness. Like many tyrants he is in essence fearful: his weakness is apparent in the language over several lines: 'faint', 'afraid', 'hint', 'hesitate', 'reserved', 'timorous', 'suspicious', 'dreading'. This emphasis makes him almost pitiable, the victim of his own surface civility. The critical failing is also a moral failing; for Pope, the two are inseparable. The portrait as a whole achieves concentration through the extended use of sharp **antitheses** which are to be found in almost every line.

The analogy with Cato is witty given that it is the title of a play written by Addison. It is also the point at which the portrait becomes funny. He and his 'little senate' are truly diminished and belittled in comparison with the Roman original, though the analogy holds: both Cato and Addison have immense pride, the one a Stoic fighting for a noble Republican cause, the other an arbiter of taste presiding over a claque of sycophantic fools. At the end, having rendered him ridiculous, the poet asks: 'Who would not laugh if such a man there be?' But this is not the last line. At the end he does not know whether simply to laugh or to cry as well. The last line names the target for the first time and there is great skill in the choice and use of the name itself.

The original Atticus was a candid friend, adviser and critic to whom the Roman writer Cicero addressed many letters. When the poet asks 'Who would not weep, if Atticus were he?' the name has great emphasis and a special charge. It does not simply identify (or mask) the historical Addison, it judges him against a true critical counterpart. It evokes an ideal which Addison has betrayed and if the English Atticus, whose talent and position is acknowledged at the beginning, is a fraud, then so much the worse for English literary culture. The use of the Roman name, therefore, artfully brings to bear a classical judgement upon the target and makes his failing a matter of national distress.

1 **John** Pope's servant, John Serle

3 **dog-star** Sirius appears in the season of the late summer heat. The associations are with madness and poetry readings in ancient Rome

4 **Bedlam** Bethlehem hospital, the madhouse
Parnassus the Greek mountain sacred to the Muses

8 **grot** his grotto running underneath the road connecting the house to his garden

10 **barge** his house was close to the river Thames

13 **Mint** a sanctuary for debtors, who were left safe from arrest elsewhere too on Sundays

18 **engross** copy a legal document

21 **Twit'nam** Twickenham

23 **Arthur** Arthur Moore, MP. His son James Smythe Moore became a poet and dramatist

25 **Cornus** a fictitious name derived from the Latin for horns, so meaning cuckold, a victim of adultery

29 *drop* or *nostrum* medicine

40 **nine years** the advice of Horace in his *Art of Poetry*, line 388

41 **Drury Lane** associated with prostitutes and starving poets

43 *term* the publishing season coincided with the legal terms

49 **Pitholeon** a foolish and pretentious poet in ancient times

50 **place** sinecure

53 **Curll** Edmund Curll (1675–1747), a disreputable and piratical publisher who might commission another libel

54 **write a Journal** become a party writer in politics or religion

61 **house** theatre

62 **Lintot** Bernard Lintot (1675–1736), Pope's publisher

66 **go snacks** share the profits

69 **Midas' ears** the ass's ears given to him by Apollo for preferring the music of Pan; he tried to hide his ears but was betrayed by his queen. Pope alludes to the king, the queen and Walpole here

85 **Codrus** a bad playwright

86 **mighty crack** alluding to Addison's infelicitous translation of the Stoic's resolve in Horace Odes, III, line 111:

Should the whole frame of nature round him break …
He unconcerned would hear the mighty crack
And stand secure amidst a falling world.

97 **Colley** Colley Cibber (1671–1757), poet laureate, later hero of *The Dunciad*

98 **Henley** a preacher who once addressed a special sermon to butchers
Moore a leading freemason of the time

99 **Bavius** a bad Roman poet

100 **Philips** Ambrose Philips, writer of pastorals, secretary to the Bishop of Armagh

101 **Sappho** Pope's name for Lady Mary Wortley Montagu, whose attack on Pope (together with Lord Hervey) precipitated this epistle

103 **twice as tall** Pope was only four foot six tall

111 **Grub Street** popular haunt of hack writers

113 **Letters** that is, in a pirated version

117 **Ammon's great son** Alexander the Great

118 **Ovid's nose** Publius Ovidius Naso (43BC–AD18), the **Augustan** poet whose last name suggests nose (nasal)

122 **Maro** the familiar name of Virgil, the greatest Roman poet. As no contemporary representations of ancient poets survive, the satire is doubly pointed

128 **numbers** verses

133 **art and care** Arbuthnot was Pope's doctor

135 **Granville** George Granville, Lord Lansdowne, to whom Pope dedicated *Windsor Forest*

136 **Walsh** an early encourager

137 **Garth** Sir Samuel Garth, author of the **mock heroic** poem *The Dispensary* (1699)

139 **courtly Talbot** Charles Talbot, Duke of Shrewsbury; all these writers had been friends of Dryden and had encouraged the young Pope

140 **mitred Rochester** Francis Atterbury, Bishop of Rochester

141 **St John** Henry, St John, Viscount Bolingbroke

146 **Burnets, Oldmixons, and Cookes** all minor writers who had attacked Pope

149 **Fanny** Lord Hervey, also 'Sporus' at line 305

151 **Gildon** Charles Gildon, a critic who attacked amongst other things *The Rape of the Lock* for its bawdiness and misuse of machinery

153 **Dennis** John Dennis attacked *An Essay on Criticism* and *The Rape of the Lock*

163 **laurel** the crown of true poets
ribbalds buffoons

164 **Bentley** Richard Bentley (1662–1742) textual critic: 'slashing' is a comment on his editorial activity
Tibbalds Lewis Theobald (pronounced as spelt by Pope), scholar and dramatist, had pointed out the deficiencies of Pope as an editor of Shakespeare, and was made hero of *The Dunciad* for his pains. His own edition of Shakespeare came out in 1734

179 **The bard** Ambrose Philips wrote derivative pastorals and a book of *Persian Tales*

180 **half-a-crown** the fee of a prostitute

190 **Tate** Nahum Tate (1651–1715), a former poet laureate of limited ability

192 **ADDISON** Joseph Addison (1672–1719), the eminent arbiter of taste, a *Spectator* editor and author of *Cato*, a tragedy on the life of the Roman Republican Stoic, for which Pope wrote a prologue. They quarrelled over the translation of Homer when Addison promoted a rival (and inferior) version of the first book of the *Iliad* by a protégé, Thomas Tickell, in 1715. Pope's response was to compose the Atticus portrait finally published here. Atticus was a Roman man of letters, friend of Cicero and later Augustus. Atticus betrays the ideal of the true critic set out in *An Essay on Criticism*

198 **the Turk** the Sultan who, it was said, on succeeding to the throne executed his brothers to secure his position

211 **templars** law students

215 **stood rubric** publishers displayed title pages in red letters, 'rubric', on billboards. These posters were called claps

222 **birthday song** the poet laureate recited a birthday ode in the presence of the king. The poetry was feeble, and George II did not like poetry anyway

225 **daggled** dragged

228 **orange** commonly sold at theatres

230 **Bufo** Latin for toad, a creature that puffs itself up with air. The portrait is a composite of notable patrons, Bubb Doddington and the Earl of Halifax
Castalian state poetry; Castalian refers to the spring on the twin-peaked mountain Parnassus, the 'forked hill', sacred to the Muses

234 **Horace and he** as a modern Maecenas, who was the great patron of Virgil and Horace

236 **Pindar** famous Greek lyric poet of the fifth century BC. The line ridicules the taste for decorative busts of poets

244 **in kind** with verses of his own

245 **Dryden** the point being that the patron fails to recognise the greatest poetic talent. Dryden had money difficulties for much of his life. At his death Halifax proposed to erect a monument to him in Westminster Abbey

250 **Bavius** may every bad poet be matched by a bad patron

256 **Gay** John Gay, friend of Pope whose epitaph was written by Pope and whose patron was the Duke of Queensberry

276 **Balbus** Viscount Dupplin who had a reputation for small talk. Balbus in Latin means stutterer

280 **Sir Will** Sir William Yonge, politician and poetaster, held in general contempt

299 **dean and *silver bell*** reference to the chapel described in Timon's villa ('Epistle to Burlington', lines 141–50). Gossip wrongly associated the villa with the Duke of Chandos's estate, Cannons

305 **Sporus** John, Lord Hervey, favourite courtier of Queen Caroline (here Eve) and Walpole who had quarrelled with Pope and attacked him in pamphlets and poems. A Roman historian records that the Emperor Nero had gone through a marriage ceremony with a eunuch called Sporus. Hervey was noted for the soft beauty of his features

306 **ass's milk** prescribed as a tonic for the delicate

319 **at the ear of Eve** see *Paradise Lost*, IV, line 800, where Satan is 'squat like a toad, close at the ear of Eve' (here Queen Caroline)
familiar as in familiar spirit or demon, supposedly in the command of a witch (here the queen)

330 **rabbins** rabbis, interpreters of scripture

331 **cherub's face** a reference to Hervey's beauty and to the depiction of the tempting serpent with an attractive human face in paintings

341 **stooped** as a falcon is said to stoop to its prey. Appropriate here when Pope
is writing of his change to satire

353 **The libelled person** attacks upon his deformity

356 **The whisper** of Lord Hervey, intimate confidant of the court

363 **Japhet** Japhet Crook, a forger convicted in 1731. He was jailed and had his
ears cut off

365 **Knight of the post** one who lived by giving false evidence for money
[knight] of the shire an MP for one of the counties

369 **Sappho** Lady Mary Wortley Montagu, a former friend now 'biting' Pope

371 **distress** the satirist (Pope) wrote a prologue to a play performed for
Dennis's benefit in 1733

373 **Moore** James Smythe Moore, who plagiarised from Pope

375 **Welsted** Leonard Welsted, a long-standing enemy of Pope. It is not certain
which particular lie Pope had in mind

378 **Budgell** accused Pope of contributing to the *Grub Street Journal*. He was
said to have forged a will in his own favour

380 **Curlls** the publisher (line 53) and Lord Hervey

391 **Bestia** a Roman consul who was bribed by the enemy into making a
dishonourable peace, perhaps referring here to the Duke of Marlborough

398 **schoolman's subtle art** scholastic casuistry

410 **a mother's breath** the lines were written in his mother's last illness. She had
in fact died by the time that the epistle was published

417 **QUEEN** Arbuthnot had been the physician of Queen Anne

THE FIRST SATIRE OF THE SECOND BOOK OF HORACE IMITATED (1733)
TO MR FORTESCUE

In a modernised version of a classic original, the poet defends his right to satirise

This was the first of a number of imitations of the Roman Augustan poet
Horace prompted by attacks made upon his satire in the *Moral Essays* (see
line 42). 'An answer from Horace was both more full and of more dignity
than any I could have made in my own person.' The imitation was an
established form made popular in the late seventeenth century in which a
poet consciously modernised a classic original, bringing it up to date with
topical allusions. The English versions were printed alongside the Latin
so that readers might appreciate the parallels.

In this dialogue, the poet who has been attacked for his satire consults a lawyer who advises him to give it up and turn instead to **panegyric** of the royal family. He declines, pointing out that they do not appreciate poetry, and goes on to say that satire is his *métier*, claiming that he uses his gift responsibly, attacking only targets that deserve it in virtue's cause. The lawyer still advises caution but when the poet distinguishes lawless libels and satires from grave epistles bringing vice to light he declares that there can be no case to answer.

In the defence of satire wittily made by Horace in dialogue with the lawyer Trebatius and wittily adapted by Pope addressing Fortescue, an old friend but supporter of the government which Pope opposed, the poet allies himself to the classical tradition in representing himself as a doughty champion of virtue against vice: satire is distinguished from libel and thus the dignity and probity of this time-honoured **genre** are vigorously asserted. As his contemporaries soon noted, Pope, in his **imitation**, is sharper and more particular in the attack than his Latin original in which Horace did not often attack recognisable living individuals. Pope's greater particularisation is not, however, the whole *raison d'être* of the satire; it is merely part of the imaginative process whereby the modern writer freely adapts to his own circumstances and purposes the sentiments and images of his ancient original.

In the original, the lawyer advises Horace to sing the praises of Augustus. Horace declines, saying that he has not the necessary talent. Pope declines on the grounds that the royal family do not appreciate poetry. He is irreverent and **ironic** at the expense of the Hanoverians and of Walpole too, so that in its political aspects the imitation subverts the original (in which Horace is in broad sympathy with the rule of Augustus) or uses the original to expose the hypocrisy of a court where poetry is not honoured, for while Horace is the unofficial laureate of the court of Augustus, George's laureate was the talentless Colley Cibber. Politically the poem signals his opposition to the ruling powers, but in addressing a Whig supporter of Walpole he is also demonstrating that, in a partisan age, his friendships and affinities cut across party lines.

But he is at one with Horace in his autobiographical candour (lines 51ff.) following in the footsteps of the free-thinking Montaigne (line 52) and claiming a detached moderation in the tradition of Erasmus (line 66). In famous lines (122–32) he adapts Roman circumstances to a version of his own life at Twickenham dedicated to gardening, friendship and 'the feast of reason and the flow of soul' (line 128). Entirely on his own terms, therefore, the poem preserves various balances, that between hurting and healing (see Critical Approaches, on Satirical Ideal & Method), between jesting and moral seriousness, between the instinct to withdraw and be detached from public affairs, cultivating one's own garden instead, and the duty to be involved in them and assume the role of public censor.

3 **Peter** Peter Walter, MP, a wealthy moneylender to the aristocracy (see line 40)

4 **Chartres** the notorious rake mentioned in the *Epistle to a Lady* (line 64)

6 **Lord Fanny** Lord Hervey

8 **counsel** Fortescue was a Whig lawyer and friend of Walpole (as well as a friend of Pope). A lawyer (Trebatius) had been addressed in the original

18 **Lettuce and cowslip-wine** to induce sleep

   probatum est it is proven, a legal phrase

19 **Celsus** the chief Roman writer on medicine

20 **Hartshorn** ammonia

21 **Caesar** ironically referring to George II

22 **bays** the laureateship, held from 1730 to 57 by Colley Cibber

23 **Sir Richard** Blackmore, author of several dull patriotic epics

24 **BRUNSWICK** George II belonged to the house of Brunswick

27 **Budgell** author of a celebration of George II whose horse had been shot from under him at the Battle of Oudenarde

31 **AMELIA** the third child of George II and Queen Caroline

34 **twice a year** at New Year and on the king's birthday. The king disliked poetry

38 **quadrille** a fashionable card game slighted in Pope's third moral essay

42 **Timon ... Balaam** Timon occurs in the *Epistle to Burlington* (lines 99ff.) and Balaam in the *Epistle to Bathurst* (lines 342ff.); both are composite portraits and therefore represented by Pope here as fictions

44 **Bond ... Harpax** a specific target and a general one. Harpax means robber

46 **Scarsdale ... Darty** a known drunkard and an epicure

47 **Ridotta** a type of society lady, derived from the Italian for a musical assembly

49 **F—** 'Fox' in the World Classics edition; probably Stephen Fox, an MP
Hockley-hole a beargarden

52 **SHIPPEN** a leading Jacobite MP admired for his honourable loyalty to his cause
Montaigne French essayist (1553–92), noted like Horace for candour and self-revelation

66 **Erasmus** Desiderius Erasmus of Rotterdam (1469–1536) who sought to unite the best of pagan culture with Christianity in an ideal of lettered piety. His humanism made him an opponent of scholasticism and church abuses satirised in his *Praise of Folly* and his *Colloquies*, subsequently put on the index of prohibited books by the Roman Catholic church. He supported reform, but a natural inclination to moderation and concord precluded full support for Luther

71 **Hectors** bullies

72 **supercargoes** officers concerned with the trade of shipping vessels (often corrupt)
directors the directors of the South Sea Company, for example, which went bankrupt in a spectacular crash causing investors (including Pope) to lose money, had been guilty of fraud

73 **Save but our *army*** a satirical thrust against the maintenance of a standing army in time of peace

75 **FLEURY** the French cardinal whose policy, like Walpole's, was peace

81 **Delia** Mary Howard, Countess of Delorain, who was supposed to have poisoned a rival in love

82 **Page** Sir Francis Page, a hard judge

83 **Sappho** Lady Mary Wortley Montagu. This couplet provoked the attack which in turn led to *An Epistle to Dr Arbuthnot*

84 **P–xed** doubly insulting; apart from the sexual reference, Lady Mary had been disfigured by smallpox

88 **Pug** a Cornish boxer

98 **whitened wall** in Bedlam, for example

99 **the Mint** a sanctuary for debtors

100 **Lee or Budgell** both poets who were insane for a time

103 **Plums** large sums of money

104 **club their testers** pool their sixpences

108 **star** the decoration for the knight of the garter

116 **unpensioned** having no income from the state, therefore independent

127 **St John** Henry St John, Viscount Bolingbroke, who in 1714 had been exiled for support of the Jacobite cause. He returned to England with a pardon in 1723 and organised Tory opposition to Walpole (see line 153). He was a friend and encourager of Pope who made him his addressee in *An Essay on Man* (see Techniques, on Rhetorical Features)

129 **Iberian lines** the Earl of Peterborough who captured Barcelona and Valencia in 1705–6

130 **quincunx** five trees, one at the centre of a square formed by the other four

145 **Richard** Richard III in whose reign a poet was executed for calling the king a hog

153 **Sir Robert** Walpole, the prime minister, to whom Pope was opposed and who took a keen interest in all writing with any political content. The passage is finely double edged. The king *might* read (but disliked poetry), bishops might write if they were honest and active in the campaign against vice, and Sir Robert would approve because he could not afford to ignore the truth

THE DUNCIAD (1743)

The goddess Dullness chooses the hero as king; games are held in honour of the goddess; the hero is transported in a vision of Elysium

(The first version of the poem in three books was published anonymously in 1728. The poem went through various stages until a final version in four books with a new hero [the poet laureate, Colley Cibber] to bring it up to date was published in 1743. The extract from Book the Second annotated and commented upon here was little changed in 1743. Line numbers are from the 1743 version.)

In the first book, the hero is chosen by the goddess Dullness and crowned king in succession to a previous favourite recently dead, thus ensuring the continuity of her reign. In the second, games are held in honour of the goddess (in parody of games held in honour of dead heroes in classical epic). In the third, the hero is transported in a vision to Elysium (paradise in the classical underworld) where the spirit of his predecessor shows him past and future triumphs of Dullness in which he will play a leading part (in parody of the vision of the glorious Roman future given to Aeneas in the underworld by the spirit of his father Anchises). In the fourth book the prophecies of the third are fulfilled.

EXTRACT FROM BOOK THE SECOND (LINES 17–120)
The dunces participate in 'high heroic games'

The goddess decrees 'high heroic games'. The dunces gather in the Strand. Publishers compete in the first race. The goddess forms the image of an insubstantial poet for the prize. The image is so like the real thing that everyone is taken in. Lintot and Curll, the two leading publishers of the day, compete for the prize. Curll slips in a puddle made by his Corinna that morning. He prays to Jove to whom Cloacina gives the prayer as he is taking his ease. His prayer is heeded, he rises and with renewed energy overtakes Lintot to win the race. He tries to seize his prize which eludes his grasp. He then tries to seize his papers but these (songs, sonnets, epigrams) are uplifted by the wind and returned to the real poets who composed them. He is left with the poet's embroidered suit but even that is taken back by the tailor who made it because he has never been paid for it. Nothing of the poet or his works remains.

In its content, this episode is a grotesque **parody** of a foot-race that occurs in both Homer and Virgil. Ajax slips upon dung in the *Iliad*, and, in the *Aeneid*, Nisus (in Virgil's adaptation of Homer) slips on the blood and filth left behind from the sacrifice, just as Curll here slides in the puddle made by his mistress Corinna. Pope himself wrote a note on this passage, partly **ironic** but also revealing his method, for an edition of the poem in 1729:

Though this incident may seem too low and base for an epic poem, the learned may very well know it to be but a copy of Homer and Virgil; the very words *onthos* [dung] and *fimus* [filth] are used by them, though our poet (in compliance with modern nicety) has remarkably enriched and coloured his language as well as raised his versification in these two episodes … it was no easy matter to invent such games as were proportioned to the meaner degree of booksellers. In Homer and Virgil, Ajax and Nisus, the persons drawn in this plight are heroes, whereas here they are such with whom it had been great impropriety to have joined any but vile ideas … Nevertheless I have often heard our author own that this part of the poem was (as frequently happens) what cost him most trouble and pleased him least, but that he hoped 'twas excusable since levelled at such as understand no delicate satire.

Pope's learned readership would have recognised the allusion to heroic games in classical epic. The enrichment of language that Pope mentions is an ironic reference to euphemism and various kinds of **periphrasis** through which the poet does not directly name what he is talking about. Much of this extract is scatological. Curll slides in a pool of urine. Jove is sitting on a celestial lavatory when his prayer is delivered by Cloacina, goddess of the sewers; the paper on which the prayers are written serves to wipe Jove's bottom. Curll is Cloacina's votary because as a publisher he figuratively trawls the sewers (he was not above publishing obscene material). At the climax of the race Curll is 'Renewed by ordure's sympathetic force'; the enriched language and stately versification are incongruously matched with the implied meaning: that he has an occult affinity with shit through which he wins the race for the non-poet. The whole passage is a figurative representation of the grubby depths to which elements in the gutter press (to use a modern cliché) will sink in their efforts to outdo each other in the race to print what proves to be empty trash. We can only admire the dexterity of Pope's **wit** in making the epic connection, translating it into comic verse and extending his **figurative language** so imaginatively.

21 **bags** bag wigs in which the hair was enclosed as in an ornamental bag
22 **crape** less expensive than silk
    garters suggesting knights of the garter
24 **hacks** hackney carriages, a common mode of transport
29 **ANNE** Queen Anne in whose reign the church of St Mary-le-Strand originated
30 **the saints of Drury Lane** Drury Lane was frequented by prostitutes
31 **stationers** booksellers
50 **More** James Smythe Moore, an insubstantial poet; the name suggests the Greek for folly
53 **Lintot** Bernard Lintot, perhaps the leading publisher of the time, published Pope's Homer
58 **Curll** Edmund Curll, a rival of Lintot in the publishing sphere and much more unscrupulous. He had published a pirated edition of Pope's letters

63 **As when a dabchick** a grotesque version of a famous passage in Milton's *Paradise Lost* (II, lines 947–50) describing Satan's progress through Chaos:

... so eagerly the fiend
O'er bog, o'er steep, through strait, rough, dense, or rare,
With head, hands, wings, or feet, pursues his way,
And swims, or sinks, or wades, or creeps, or flies.

70 **Corinna** the name that the Roman poet Ovid gave his mistress
73 **Here fortuned Curll to slide** see comment on this episode above
78 **caitiff vaticide** base murderer of poets
82 **the Pope's Arms** the Bible is Curll's sign, the cross keys, as in the papal crown, Lintot's
84 **Ambrosia** the solid food of the gods
92 **Ichor** the blood of the gods
93 **Cloacina** the purifier, the Roman goddess of the common shores
98 **black grottos** coal wharves on the Thames
100 **link-boys** boys who carried torches in the streets to light the way
116 **Evans, Young and Swift** wits, not dunces

PART THREE

CRITICAL APPROACHES

THEMES

POETRY & ENLIGHTENMENT

Although Pope's literary career spans some 40 years and involved him in the composition of a wide variety of poems, there is a remarkable coherence of underlying theme and viewpoint. This coherence stems from a clutch of interlocking core beliefs, the ground of which may be suggested in the following injunction delivered by the poet to the would-be critic in *An Essay on Criticism* (1711):

> First follow *Nature*, and your judgment frame
> By her just standard, which is still the same:
> Unerring NATURE, still divinely bright,
> One clear, unchanged, and universal light,
> Life, force, and beauty, must to all impart,
> At once the source, and end, and test of art. (lines 68–73)

Here is Pope's belief in the underlying order that gives dignity, beauty and meaning to the cosmos. This is a metaphysical concept, expressed through the figure of a 'light' which is 'divinely bright', 'clear', 'universal' and 'unchanged'. Light is a recurring **metaphor** in *An Essay on Criticism* as it is elsewhere in Pope's poetry. It occurs most crucially to define the nature of true expression:

> But true expression, like th' unchanging sun
> Clears, and improves whate'er it shines upon,
> It gilds all objects, but it alters none.
> (*An Essay on Criticism*, lines 315–17)

True expression is enlightening. The poet does not mean here that artistic expression offers an improved version of reality which comforts us because it is what we might wish our own to be, for true expression does not alter objects: it simply presents them in a clearer light. The lily is not gilded but revealed in all its natural beauty. It is our perception through

the superior clarity of the artist's vision that is improved. The root idea is
that it is the sacred function of art to throw the universal into a clear
radiant light and the sacred duty of the artist to render and express his
vision with emphatic clarity.

This is a lofty conception of the nature and function of artistic
expression. It suggests the light in which Pope's famous definition of **wit**
(imaginative literature) should be read:

> True wit is nature to advantage dressed;
>
> What oft was thought, but ne'er so well expressed;
>
> Something, whose truth convinced at sight we find,
>
> That gives us back the image of our mind.
>
> (*An Essay on Criticism*, lines 297–300)

These lines are capable of a banal interpretation. But the first couplet is
not **end-stopped**; its sense carries over into the next and when it is related
to what is said of nature and expression in the *Essay* it is apparent that it
means rather more than that poetry is nothing but the polished
expression of commonplace notions.

Enlightenment in vital matters is essentially a gift, a light that the
individual must perceive from within, as the poet advises us when passing
on hints from the Earl of Burlington on the topic of architecture and
landscape gardening. No rule book, even from the great and the good,
can teach good **sense** which for Pope is the ground of all success:

> Something there is, more needful than expense,
>
> And something previous ev'n to taste – 'tis sense:
>
> Good sense, which only is the gift of heaven,
>
> And though no science, fairly worth the seven:
>
> A light, which in yourself you must perceive;
>
> Jones and Le Nôtre have it not to give.
>
> (*Epistle to Burlington*, lines 41–6)

The language here suggests that for Pope good sense is no humdrum
virtue. Samuel Johnson, speaking of Pope himself, offers an illuminating
definition: 'Of his intellectual character, the constituent and fundamental
principle was good sense, a prompt and intuitive perception of
consonance and propriety.' Such an intuitive perception is not a science
that can be learnt.

Modern science, though, can throw a good deal of light upon the cosmos, a notion wittily clarified in Pope's epitaph on the physicist Isaac Newton (1642–1727), who explained the composition of white light and is famous for his work on the laws of motion: 'Nature and Nature's Laws lay hid in Night: / GOD said, '*Let Newton be!*' and all was Light!' Where, in the earlier seventeenth century, new scientific discovery had often caused doubt and uncertainty, in the later part of the seventeenth and the early eighteenth century scientific progress was not necessarily seen to conflict with traditional religion but confirmed the divinely ordained plan now being newly discovered by human intelligence.

Scientific progress also led to a growing optimism about the growth of human understanding and man's ability to control his destiny. Some of this confidence is reflected in the poetry of Pope and is particularly prevalent in *An Essay on Man* in which the poet's purpose is to 'vindicate the ways of God to Man' ('Epistle I', line 16). This echoes the grand argument of John Milton (1608–74) in his epic poem on the Fall of Man, *Paradise Lost* (1667), 'that I may assert eternal Providence, and justify the ways of God to man' (Book One, lines 25–6). But Pope's vindication makes no mention of the traditional biblical story of creation which had been the basis of Milton's epic or even of the divine revelation through the life of Christ, but seeks to argue that 'WHATEVER IS, IS RIGHT' (Epistle IV, line 394) by philosophic means. Theology is replaced by reason and philosophy.

Yet, although his poetry in its disciplined regularity may be said to give expression to the values of the European **Enlightenment**, Pope also brings a more traditional perspective to bear upon the new scientific Enlightenment. Of Newton he asks in *An Essay on Man*:

> Could he, whose rules the rapid Comet bind,
> Describe or fix one movement of his Mind?
> Who saw its fires here rise, and there descend,
> Explain his own beginning, or his end?
> (Epistle II, lines 35–8)

The highest value is set upon enlightening human reason:

> Pride, where wit fails, steps in to our defence,
> And fills up all the mighty void of sense.

> If once right reason drive that cloud away,
> Truth breaks upon us with resistless day.
> (*An Essay on Criticism*, lines 209–12)

But the juxtapositioning of reason here with the old vice of pride reminds us of the formidable obstacles that get in the way of the exercising of right reason in human affairs.

As the age of Pope has often been called the Age of Reason and Pope has sometimes been called its poet, it will be worth examining what he has to say about the limits of human reason, illustrated in a well known passage which encapsulates much of his general view of humanity from *An Essay on Man*:

> Know then thyself, presume not God to scan;
> The proper study of Mankind is Man.
> Plac'd on this isthmus of a middle state,
> A Being darkly wise, and rudely great:
> With too much knowledge for the Sceptic side,
> With too much weakness for the Stoic's pride,
> He hangs between; in doubt to act, or rest;
> In doubt to deem himself a God, or Beast;
> In doubt his Mind or Body to prefer;
> Born but to die, and reas'ning but to err;
> Alike in ignorance, his reason such,
> Whether he thinks too little, or too much:
> Chaos of Thought and Passion, all confus'd;
> Still by himself abus'd, or disabus'd;
> Created half to rise, and half to fall;
> Great lord of all things, yet a prey to all;
> Sole judge of Truth, in endless Error hurl'd;
> The glory, jest, and riddle of the world!
> (Epistle II, lines 1–18)

What stands out here is the emphasis upon human limitation reflected in doubt (repeated three times), error, ignorance and chaos. Man is 'A Being *darkly* wise, and *rudely* great' (my italic); his wisdom is incomplete (there may be an echo of St Paul's phrase in his first letter to the Corinthians 'for now we see through a glass darkly' (13.11)) and his greatness is imperfect and flawed. The emphasis in these **oxymoronic** couplings falls very much on the qualifying adverbs which suggest limitation. He is neither a god nor a beast but something in between. This is a traditional vision of man occupying a middle place in the great Chain of Being. But humanity does not thereby occupy a comfortable position. It is caught between the conflicting claims of mind and body, thought and passion. The balance in the lines comes down to stress confusion, falling off, vulnerability and violent displacement. Man may be the world's glory, but he is also ridiculous and a mystery to himself. The poet poses but does not solve the riddle. There is complexity and perplexity here. However much he may have believed the universe to be an expression of divine reason, Pope's evocation in these lines of the **paradoxical** character of man (achieved through a masterly balancing of opposites in the condensed dialectic of the **Augustan** couplet) hardly suggests that his poetry will express an easy confidence in the capacity of human beings for rational action or an uncritical faith in the products of human reason.

In fact these lines which identify what is the proper study for mankind provide the context for understanding his dismissal of various forms of what he regarded as unenlightening science, improper study, in the *Dunciad*. He is wary of 'pure' science that is not clearly related to human ends when he **satirises** botanists and shell collectors. It is not only natural science that attracts satiric attention but also the minute work of scholars analysing texts. Telling here is the use of a scientific instrument, the microscope, which is used to illustrate a distortion in vision on the part of those who have no eyes for the larger picture.

> The critic Eye, that microscope of Wit,
> Sees hairs and pores, examines bit by bit:
> How parts relate to parts, or they to whole,
> The body's harmony, the beaming soul,
> Are things which Kuster, Burman, Wasse shall see
> When man's whole frame is obvious to a *Flea*.
> (*Dunciad* IV, lines 233–8)

In *The Dunciad* at large the force and effect of dullness are 'To blot out Order and extinguish Light' (IV, line 14). The goddess dullness undoes creation: 'Light dies before thy uncreating word' (IV, line 654) and the result of her triumph at the end is that 'universal Darkness buries All' (IV, line 656). It is perhaps **ironic** that one of the most powerful visions of the enlightened poet should be a negative vision of encroaching cultural gloom and desolation.

Distrust of the new science, apparent in the use of the microscope, may be paralleled in the unfavourable light cast by the prism in *An Essay on Criticism*:

> False eloquence, like the prismatic glass,
> Its gaudy colours spreads on every place;
> The face of nature we no more survey,
> All glares alike, without distinction gay. (lines 311–4)

Pope casts a cold eye on the new scientific rationalism of the enlightenment. Nevertheless, the energy with which the negative vision of darkness and disorder is envisaged was only made possible by the strength of the poet's belief in the universal light of Nature. Pope is both the foremost poet of the enlightenment and **paradoxically** its greatest critic.

THE POET OF MANNERS & SOCIAL CRITIC

Pope's poetry engages closely with the social life of its times. He is largely concerned with life at the top, an upper-class world centred upon the London life of the aristocracy. Queen Anne herself presides at Hampton Court where the cutting of the lock takes place. Many of his poems are addressed to aristocrats such as Lord Bolingbroke and the Earl of Burlington. Duchesses feature in the *Epistle to a Lady* along with Lady Mary Wortley Montagu. These aristocrats, who still rule the land in the early eighteenth century, may be the subject of praise (Burlington and Bolingbroke) or censure (Lord Hervey and Lady Mary); the poet is not conducting any kind of class war in his satire but exhibiting a moralist's general concern with human behaviour as it is exhibited in particular examples. Recognised as the leading man of letters almost from the start of his career, Pope had access to this upper-class world, made friends from it and made it the subject of his poetry because it was the world he knew and because its behaviour and taste were central to the health and well-being of the nation.

In view of the emphasis upon the female sex in *The Rape of the Lock* and the *Epistle to a Lady* it perhaps needs to be said that Pope, who in life had a number of female friends and left his property to Martha Blount (the lady of the epistle), is not unsympathetic to the position of women in his society, only to 'society ladies' (see further comment on this in relation to the portrait of Cloe in Extended Commentaries, Text 3): 'Too much your Sex is by their forms confin'd / Severe to all, but most to Womankind' ('Epistle to Miss Blount, with the Works of Voiture', lines 31–2).

In a world where independence and a career were possibilities hardly available to women, Pope invites prudent thought about the critical choice of life facing contemporary women. In this epistle, addressed to Martha Blount, the negative example has wished for superficial things and made the wrong choice.

> The gods, to curse Pamela with her pray'rs,
> Gave the gilt Coach and dappled Flanders Mares,
> The shining robes, rich jewels, beds of state,
> And, to complete her bliss, a Fool for Mate.
> She glares in Balls, front Boxes, and the Ring,
> A vain, unquiet, glitt'ring, wretched Thing!
> Pride, pomp, and State but reach her outward part;
> She sighs, and is no Duchess at her heart. (lines 49–56)

There are different attitudes to the same fashionable social world in different poems. The poet is genial and **ironic** in the 'Epistle to Miss Blount, on her leaving the Town after the Coronation', gently mocking in *The Rape of the Lock* and severely ridiculing in *Epistle to a Lady* (for further discussion, see Extended Commentaries in which these three poems feature).

THE LITERARY CRITIC & STANDARD-BEARER OF CULTURAL VALUES

Pope was confident in his poetic talent from an early age. In *An Essay on Criticism* (1711) he took up the mantle of the poet-critic, like the Roman Horace before him in his *Art of Poetry*, and began there a campaign for high standards in poetry and criticism that remained one of the great themes of his life and literary output.

> Horace still charms with graceful negligence,
> And without method talks us into sense,
> Will, like a friend, familiarly convey
> The truest notions in the easiest way.
> He, who supreme in judgment, as in wit,
> Might boldly censure, as he boldly writ,
> Yet judged with coolness, though he sung with fire;
> His precepts teach but what his works inspire. (lines 653–60)

The first four lines here describe the style and manner of Horace that Pope made his own in his verse epistles and **moral essays**. The last four describe the special authority that is owed to the criticism of the practising poet. Here too in the Horatian ideal is a paradoxical blend of opposites, uniting the cool judgement of the critic with the creative fire of the poet. Emulation of Horace remained an abiding theme in Pope's life.

The principles that Pope gave voice to in this early *Essay* he put into practice in a personal defence of his own literary career twenty-five years later in *An Epistle to Dr Arbuthnot* (1735). In *The Dunciad* (first published in 1728, then re-issued with a new hero in 1743) he offered in serio-comic form a negative critique of the cultural life of his times. In his moral essays of the 1730s (such as the *Epistle to Burlington* on taste in architecture and gardening) and his Horatian imitations, he further campaigned for high standards in cultural life based upon self-knowledge in individuals, satirical exposure of the dull and venal, and positive identification of creative talent and moral worth in contemporary life. In the 'Epistle to Augustus' of 1737, he wrote impersonally (unlike *Arbuthnot*) and specifically (in contrast to the more general *Essay on Criticism*) on the literary life of his times, passing judgements on contemporary culture and, like Horace before him, powerfully campaigning for the moderns against those who denigrated modern literature in favour of the ancients (see Literary Background, on The Augustan Age).

SATIRICAL IDEAL & METHOD

In his 'Epistle to Augustus', in imitation of the verse epistle addressed by the Roman poet Horace to Emperor Augustus (see Literary

Background), Pope, like Horace before him, aims to assert the civic utility of poetry and traces the origin of satire to innocent jesting at country festivals; when holiday licence turned malicious, legal restraint became necessary, turning most poets away from jesting towards flattery but the more discriminating were able to distinguish between liberty and licence: 'Hence Satire rose, that just the medium hit, / And heals with Morals what it hurts with Wit' (*The First Epistle of the Second Book of Horace Imitated*, lines 261–2).

In this justification of satire, Pope is at one with Horace in asserting an ideal, a moral balance between hurting and healing in which **wit** is not indulged in to delight itself but is subject to restraint and serves a moral purpose. In pursuit of such an ideal medium, Pope developed the moral essay, a blend of satire and **panegyric** (praise of an individual), in which the positive healing element is fully explicit as it often is in the satires and epistles of Horace. Both poets characteristically conduct a moral dialogue, usually with a specific addressee (for example, Martha Blount, the woman of sense in the *Epistle to a Lady* and the tasteful Earl of Burlington in the epistle that bears his name), and through the addressee with the reader. Poet, addressee and reader are all implicated in a set of civilised values that are defined, asserted and represented in the style and conduct of the poem. In other satires, the positive is not far to seek. In *An Epistle to Dr Arbuthnot* it is the poet who speaks in his own voice to defend himself at the close. In the Horatian **imitations**, Pope associates himself with the ideas of the good life he found in Horace and consciously makes them appropriate to his own style of living at Twickenham:

> Know, all the distant din that world can keep,
> Rolls o'er my grotto and but soothes my sleep.
> There, my retreat the best companions grace,
> Chiefs out of war, and statesmen out of place.
> There ST JOHN mingles with my friendly bowl
> The feast of reason and the flow of soul:
> (*The First Satire of the Second Book of Horace Imitated*, lines 123–8)

Towards the end of his career, his satire became increasingly particular and personal in its attack. His friend Dr Arbuthnot feared for his safety and urged him not to be so combative. In his prose reply, Pope defends the use of particular example:

To reform and not to chastise I am afraid is impossible. The best precepts as well as the best laws, would prove of small use if there was no example to enforce them. To attack vices in the abstract, without touching persons, may be safe fighting indeed, but it is fighting with shadows. General propositions are obscure, misty, and uncertain, compared with plain, full and home examples [examples near home]. Precepts only apply to our reason, which in most men is but weak; examples are pictures, and strike the senses, nay raise the passions, and call in those (the strongest and most general of all motives) to the aid of reformation. Every vicious man makes the case his own; and that is the only way by which such men can be affected, much less deterred. So that to chastise is to reform. The only sign by which I found my writings ever did any good, or had any weight, has been that they raised the anger of bad men. And my greatest comfort and encouragement to proceed has been to see that those who have no shame and no fear of anything else have appeared touched by my satires.

In the verse *Epistle to Dr Arbuthnot*, he acknowledges a weakness in this theory. When the satirist announces an intention to attack Sporus, the interlocutor (the good Doctor himself) is made to interrupt with the objection that Sporus has so little sense of proportion that he will neither understand nor heed the satire.

> Let Sporus tremble – 'What? that thing of silk,
> Sporus, that mere white curd of ass's milk?
> Satire or sense, alas! can Sporus feel?
> Who breaks a butterfly upon a wheel?'
>   Yet let me flap this bug with gilded wings,
> This painted child of dirt, that stinks and stings; (lines 305–10)

The victim will not be affected, but the satirist will continue anyway and goes on to paint a most darkly passionate portrait in which the gilded courtier and would-be wit, is imaginatively transformed through the use of animal imagery and Satanic association and by the concentrated application of Pope's favourite **rhetorical** figure (see below) into something that is the reverse of what it seems to be: 'one vile antithesis' (line 325). We may admire the art, as did Lord Byron (1788–1824):

> Now is there a line in all the passage without the most forceful imagery (for his purpose)? Look at the variety, at the poetry, of the passage – at the imagination, there is hardly a line from which a painting might not be made and *is*.

Or the thought that an actual figure is submerged in the portrait may make us uneasy, prompting the ultimately unanswerable question: was Pope fair? Samuel Johnson, who admired the elegance, spirit and dignity of the poet's vindication of his own character at the close of the epistle, nevertheless concluded: 'The meanest passage is the satire on Sporus.'

While admiring the persuasive arts of Pope in *An Epistle to Dr Arbuthnot*, many have been prompted by its often strident tone to wonder what relation the self-dramatisation there of the talented and forbearing poet beset by fools and malignant critics bears to the facts of the case. It is one thing to ask whether the image of the poet is persuasive and credible, another to ask whether it is entirely honest and true. If we desire an answer to the second question, we must go beyond the poem itself, to the life of the poet and the history of the times in which he lived. In his *Life*, Johnson, while admiring Pope's art and applauding his genius, does not gloss over what he considers to be defects in his character, pointing to a tendency in Pope to deception of himself and others, to affectation, snobbery and aggression in dispute. He admired *The Dunciad* as 'the best specimen that has yet appeared of personal satire ludicrously pompous' but was not convinced that its design was moral, feeling that it owed its origin in part to petulance and malignancy in Pope.

Pope himself asserted the integrity of his intentions: 'Ask you what provocation I have had? / The strong antipathy of good to bad ('Epilogue to the Satires', Dialogue II, lines 197–8).

It would be churlish not to recognise a ruling passion here. But was he always undeceived? What of the morals of the moralist? In judging his particular character we may bear in mind his own general account of the elusive **paradox** of human character when judging and when judged, in his *Epistle to Lord Cobham*:

> Know, GOD and NATURE only are the same:
> In Man, the judgment shoots at flying game;
> A bird of passage! gone as soon as found,
> Now in the Moon, perhaps, now under ground. (lines 95–8)

As judges, the poet argues, we are prevented from seeing the object clearly because our vision is coloured by our own passions and imagination:

All Manners take a tincture from our own;

Or come discolour'd thro' our Passions shown.

Or Fancy's beam enlarges, multiplies,

Contracts, inverts, and gives ten thousand dyes. (lines 33–6)

We often do not know our own motives: 'Oft in the Passions' wild rotation tost / Our spring of action to ourselves is lost' (lines 41–2). Even the best lives are deceptive: 'Unthought-of Frailties cheat us in the Wise' (line 69). This is part of the more general puzzle involving radical human inconsistency wherein: 'The rogue and fool by fits is fair and wise; / And ev'n the best, by fits, what they despise' (*An Essay on Man*, II, lines 233–4). We owe it to the author of these lines not to take a simple view.

TECHNIQUES

REFINEMENT OF THE HEROIC COUPLET

Almost all Pope's poems are written in couplets, the rhymed **iambic pentameter**, a form that predominated in the period between 1660 and 1780. Milton's use of **blank verse** (the unrhymed iambic pentameter) for *Paradise Lost* is exceptional. Long before Pope the couplet had been organised into its characteristic **Neoclassical** form, **end-stopped** with strong rhymes and a balanced **rhetorical** structure. The ideal to which Neoclassical writers aspired is famously expressed in a couplet composed in imitation of the Thames by John Denham (1615–69) in his topographical poem *Cooper's Hill* (1642). Denham first hails the Thames as his example, wishing he could produce verse that runs with the river's majestic flow and then characterises in his verse the qualities he admires in the Thames:

Oh could I flow like thee, and make thy stream

My great example as it is my theme!

Though deep, yet clear, though gentle yet not dull;

Strong without rage, without o'er-flowing full. (lines 189–92)

These lines became famous in the period and were much quoted and imitated, for the description of the Thames is organised in such a way that it becomes a **figurative** expression defining a stylistic ideal. Denham here succeeds in his aspiration to write in language that has depth but is not obscure (it is both literal and figurative), that is smooth flowing but varied enough not to fall into too regular a pattern (the breaks in the lines are in different places), that has a controlled strength (it is emphatic without containing exaggeration), and that is self-contained in a unit in which every word counts (with no enjambement). It beautifully evokes the river and embodies the style to which it aspires at the same time. The structure of its clauses makes it a very classical instrument, if the term classical implies pattern, regularity, order and balance.

The youthful Pope gave much thought to the composition of couplets as the following letter addressed to one of his mentors in 1710 testifies. To a modern view it may seem that he is concerned with trivialities for much of the time. Yet there is material for reflection here. Most readers will concede that the Neoclassical couplet is an artful form but a common reaction is that couplet writing can become wearisome because of its sameness, its regularity. What follows suggests that the deliberate regularity (literally a state achieved through the application of rules) was directed towards two particular effects: the avoidance of ugly sounds and the achievement of *variety*. The minuteness of the following observations suggests that the ears of Pope and his readers were sensitively attuned in ways that most of us can scarcely appreciate. If writing couplets is an art, then so is reading them. It needs practice. To use a musical analogy, chamber music to the uninitiated ear may all sound the same. It is only with repeated listening that the ear begins to penetrate the general idiom and comes to discriminate variations within the idiom appreciatively. The same might be said of Bach cantatas, Mozart operas, or various kinds of rock music.

> 1. As to the hiatus [the break between two vowels coming together without an intervening consonant], it is certainly to be avoided as often as possible; but on the other hand, since the reason of it is only for the sake of the numbers [the metre], so if to avoid it we incur another fault against their smoothness, methinks the very end of that nicety [precise requirement] is destroyed. As when we say (for instance):
>
> > But th'old have interest ever in their view
>
> to avoid the hiatus in 'The old have interest,' does not the ear in this place tell us that the hiatus is smoother, less constrained, and so preferable to the caesura [cutting of the vowel].

2. I would except all expletives in verse, as 'do' before verbs plural, or even too frequent use of 'did' and 'does', to change the termination of the rhyme, all these being against the usual manner of speech and mere fillers-up of unnecessary syllables.

3. Monosyllable-lines, unless very artfully managed are stiff, languishing, and hard.

4. The repeating the same rhymes within four or six lines of each other, which tire the ear with too much like sound.

5. The two frequent use of Alexandrines [a line of six feet or twelve syllables as opposed to five feet and ten syllables], which are never graceful but when there is some majesty added to the verse by them, or when there cannot be found a word in them but what is absolutely needful.

6. Every nice [discriminating] ear must (I believe) have observed that in any smooth English verse of ten syllables there is naturally a pause at the fourth, fifth, or sixth syllable, as for example, Waller:

> At the fifth: Where'er thy navy / spreads her canvas wings
> At the fourth: Homage to thee / and peace to all she brings.
> At the sixth: like tracks of leverets / in morning snow.

Now I fancy that to preserve an exact harmony and variety none of these pauses should be continued above three lines together without the interposition of another; else it will be apt to weary the ear with one continued tone; at least it does mine.

7. It is not enough that nothing offends the ear, that the verse be (as the French call it) *coulante* ['flowing']; but a good poet will adapt the very sounds, as well as the words, to the things he treats of. So that there is (if one may express it so) a Style of Sound: as in describing a gliding stream the numbers should run easy and flowing, in describing a rough torrent or deluge, sonorous and swelling, and so of the rest.

This last requirement moves beyond minutiae to something larger, the doctrine of imitative or representational harmony. Pope went on to give examples of what he means in the following lines in *An Essay on Criticism*:

> True ease in writing comes from art, not chance,
> As those move easiest who have learned to dance.
> 'Tis not enough no harshness gives offence,
> The sound must seem an echo to the sense:
> Soft is the strain when Zephyr gently blows,

> And the smooth stream in smoother numbers flows;
> But when loud surges lash the sounding shore,
> The hoarse, rough verse should like the torrent roar.
> When Ajax strives some rock's vast weight to throw,
> The line too labours, and the words move slow:
> Not so, when swift Camilla scours the plain,
> Flies o'er the unbending corn, and skims along the main. (lines 362–73)

Pope is aiming to imitate smoothness and roughness in the rhythm and movement of the verse itself. In another example, the strain is soft and smooth when Belinda is sailing down the Thames:

> But now secure the painted vessel glides,
> The sunbeams trembling on the floating tides;
> While melting music steals upon the sky,
> And softened sounds along the waters die;
> Smooth flow the waves, the zephyrs gently play,
> Belinda smiled, and all the world was gay.
> (*The Rape of the Lock*, Canto II, lines 47–52)

When the fighting begins, the rhythm is broken and the sounds are harsh:

> 'To arms, to arms!' the fierce virago cries,
> And swift as lightning to the combat flies.
> All sides in parties, and begin th' attack.
> Fans clap, silks rustle, and tough whalebones crack;
> (*The Rape of the Lock*, Canto V, lines 37–40)

Dull couplet writing is wittily exemplified and mocked in the *Essay*:

> These equal syllables alone require,
> Though oft the ear the open vowels tire;
> While expletives their feeble aid do join;
> And ten low words oft creep in one dull line:
> While they ring round the same unvaried chimes,
> With sure returns of still expected rhymes;
> Wher-e'er you find 'the cooling western breeze,'
> In the next line, it 'whispers through the trees':
> If crystal streams 'with pleasing murmurs creep',

> The reader's threatened (not in vain) with 'sleep.'
> Then, at the last and only couplet fraught
> With some unmeaning thing they call a thought,
> A needless Alexandrine ends the song,
> That, like a wounded snake, drags its slow length along.
> (*An Essay on Criticism*, lines 344–57)

There are three open vowels in the second line, an expletive 'do' in the third, ten low words in the next, an unenergetic monosyllabic line. Then he makes fun of clichéed rhymes and exemplifies the Alexandrine twice for emphasis. The 'unmeaning thing' finally drags itself along in a line of slow snakiness, emphasised by the collocation of sounds at the end.

Although he values '**correctness**', that is, writing that is highly polished and obeys all the rules, he also ridicules those who cannot go beyond it:

> But in such lays as neither ebb, nor flow,
> Correctly cold, and regularly low,
> That shunning faults, one quiet tenor keep;
> We cannot blame indeed – but we may sleep. (lines 239–42)

Pope's aesthetic ideal as realised in the landscape of *Windsor Forest* expresses his ideal of the couplet rather as Denham had realised and expressed his ideal through the Thames:

> Here hills and vales, the woodland and the plain,
> Here earth and water seem to strive again;
> Not chaos-like together crushed and bruised,
> But as the world, harmoniously confused:
> Where order in variety we see,
> And where, though all things differ, all agree.
> (*Windsor Forest*, lines 11–16)

It might be argued that the couplet form as ordered by Pope encapsulates a way of looking at the world and is the linguistic or rhetorical representation of a belief and conviction about the nature of the universe. The couplet itself is a kind of *harmonia discors*, a harmony made from discordant elements, in which all the world's variety is contained in a harmonious order. **Paradoxically**, too much regularity, by smoothing out the discord from which it is made, betrays this harmony.

Refinement of the heroic couplet continued

This aesthetic underlies too his own informal style of gardening put into practice at Twickenham and it is from the same aesthetic perspective that he makes his recommendations in the *Epistle to Burlington*:

> To build, to plant, whatever you intend,
> To rear the column, or the arch to bend,
> To swell the terrace, or to sink the grot,
> In all, let nature never be forgot,
> But treat the goddess like a modest fair,
> Nor over-dress, nor leave her wholly bare;
> Let not each beauty everywhere be spied,
> Where half the skill is decently to hide.
> He gains all points, who pleasingly confounds,
> Surprises, varies, and conceals the bounds. (lines 47–56)

Timon's Villa, on the other hand, is the inverse of this aesthetic, representing the dull uniformity of a rigid eighteenth-century classicism:

> His gardens next your admiration call,
> On every side you look, behold the wall!
> No pleasing intricacies intervene,
> No artful wildness to perplex the scene:
> Grove nods at grove, each alley has a brother,
> And half the platform just reflects the other.
> (*Epistle to Burlington*, lines 113–18)

The regular symmetry of the landscaping is brilliantly mocked in the form and metrical arrangement of the final couplet. The final line in which half the platform (a raised terrace) exactly reflects the other is wittily split exactly into two with a break after five syllables and so mimics the symmetry it is mocking.

The practical effects of 'correctness' in Pope can best be appreciated when we can find evidence of Pope's correcting himself, that is, polishing up and improving lines in a subsequent revision. *The Rape of the Lock* was first published in a two-canto version in 1712 and then after its successful reception greatly expanded to its present five cantos in 1714. There is a considerable overlap between the two versions. Many of the lines from 1712 are simply reproduced in 1714. But some lines and couplets are modified, as in the following examples:

And dwells such rage in softest bosoms then?
And lodge such daring souls in little men? (Canto I, lines 11–12: 1712)

In tasks so bold, can little men engage,
And in soft bosoms dwell such mighty rage? (Canto I, 11–12: 1714)

The couplet juxtaposes the boldness of the Baron in seizing the lock with the rage of Belinda when it is taken. Since the boldness provokes the rage, the order of the second version, which puts the cause before the effect, is logically more satisfying and gives due emphasis, where it is needed in the final rhyme word, to the ensuing mighty rage that caused the breach between the families and so prompted Pope to write the poem. The rage, which we cannot miss in 1714 because of the emphatic climax of the rhyme word, is secondary in 1712 to the belittling of the Baron. The rhyming of *then* with *men* does not deliver anything as emphatic as the rhyming of *engage* with *rage*. The 1712 version is good enough in itself until we have read the improvement. With the emphatic reordering of the rhyme, the whole couplet becomes crisper and more pointed, delivering an epigrammatic clarity.

Interestingly, most of Pope's rhyme words are verbs and nouns, pointing to some important action or highlighting some person, thing, or – as here – emotion. And the Neoclassical couplet, in which the vast majority of rhyme words are monosyllabic habitually has rhymes that by virtue of their strength and emphasis are called **masculine rhymes**. In the whole of *The Rape of the Lock*, there are only some twenty couplets where both rhyme words are dissyllables (have two syllables) and there are hardly any dissyllables used where the stress does not fall naturally on the final syllable. There are only about twenty trissyllabic (three-syllable) rhyme words in a poem of some 750 lines. If a **feminine rhyme** is defined as a rhyme where the stress in both rhyme words falls on the penultimate syllable, then there is only one feminine rhyme in *The Rape of the Lock*, which is included for a special echoing and delaying effect at the climax of the poem's action: 'The meeting points the sacred hair dissever, / From the fair head, for ever, and for ever!' (Canto III, lines 153–4).

In a weak poet the rhymes will often be awkward and dictate the sense; a good poet uses the rhymes to clarify and give emphasis to his meaning. Here the finality of the climactic event of the poem and its melodrama is intensified by the doubly chiming rhyme.

Something of the same is true of the following improvement:

> Sol through white curtains did his beams display
> And oped those eyes which brighter shine than they. (Canto I, lines 13–4: 1712)

> Sol through white curtains shot a timorous ray
> And oped those eyes that must eclipse the day. (Canto I, lines 13–4: 1714)

The rhyme words in 1714 make the utterance more pointed, emphasising the light by the repetition in the two nouns 'ray' and 'day'. Pope in the reordering of 1714 has rid himself of an expletive 'did'; every single word now counts. But the most significant change is not to do with the rhyme words or with something that is just superficial; he has intensified the underlying **wit** of the couplet. Both versions offer extravagant praise of the beauty of Belinda's eyes by means of an exaggeration, an **hyperbole**, which compares their brightness to that of the sun (Sol, the Latin word for sun) which is personified here. But in 1714, the poet makes greater use of the personification by making the sun's ray 'timorous' and introduces a bolder **metaphor**, 'eclipse', in the revision. The sun is afraid because he does not want to be eclipsed. The compliment to the power of Belinda's beauty is enhanced. The improved version has greater artifice but through the artifice delivers its sense more wittily and emphatically.

Rhetorical features

Although we are wary of the term today, almost all poetry before the modernists of the early twentieth century consciously turned against it has a strong **rhetorical** element. Rhetoric (from the Greek word *rhetor*, a speaker) is simply the art of speaking and writing effectively; the organisation of what the speaker or writer wants to say in such a way as to be emphatic and compel attention. It existed before it was described and is as old as poetry itself. The Greek epic poet Homer, with whom the western poetic tradition may be said to begin, filled more than half of the *Iliad* with speeches in which all the main devices of rhetoric are deployed. Subsequently grammarians identified these devices, gave them names and produced manuals describing and illustrating their effects and extending their analysis beyond speeches to any kind of narrative. This knowledge soon became automatically part of any programme which sought to teach the art of speaking or writing and was imbibed by school children at an early age. Renaissance poetry is highly rhetorical; Shakespeare is a rhetorical dramatist in the sense that he exploits the devices of Elizabethan rhetoric, which he doubtless learned at Stratford grammar school, in the dramatic speeches of his characters.

In the history of rhetoric, a useful distinction has often (though not invariably) been made between what have been called figures of sense and figures of arrangement or sound. In the former case, language is not used in a literal sense but turned from the literal into the nonliteral, or figurative. These figures of sense are often called *tropes* from the Greek word for 'turn' or 'turning', to reflect this turning away from the literal sense towards something other. The most obvious figures in this category are the **metaphor** and **simile**. Figures of sound, such alliteration, assonance and consonance, do not change meaning but make the phrases in which they occur more memorable or emphatic. Figures of arrangement, like **antithesis** and **anaphora**, involving syntax, sentence structure and word order, may affect meaning but do not usually turn the literal into the nonliteral. They are used for emphasis and clarity. Hard and fast distinctions cannot always be maintained as a few figures, like **zeugma** (see below) may be described both as figures of sense and of arrangement. **Figurative language** is therefore not simply metaphorical language (today the phrase is often narrowed to this meaning), but any kind of artfully organised utterance. The Greek and Latin names given to the various figures (rhetoricians have identified hundreds) reflect their initial discovery and description by the Greeks and Romans in their rhetorical schools and manuals.

Pope is a master of rhetoric which he deploys with the greatest artistry in the couplet form. As was apparent in the couplets of Denham on the Thames, the Neoclassical couplet particularly encourages a balanced pattern of arrangement. In Pope as in Denham, one of its commonest figures is the antithesis, the opposing of contrasting ideas within and between lines of the closed couplet. In his satirical portrait of Sporus, the false courtier, Pope makes his target the embodiment of his favourite figure which is exemplified in an intense see-saw display that both precedes and follows it:

> His wit all seesaw, between *that* and *this*,
> Now high, now low, now master up, now miss.

> And he himself one vile antithesis.
> Amphibious thing! that acting either part,
> The trifling head, or the corrupted heart,
> Fop at the toilet, flatterer at the board,
> Now trips a lady, now struts a lord.
> (*An Epistle to Dr Arbuthnot*, lines 323–33)

There are three antitheses in the first couplet and three strong oppositions in the last three lines. The first three point to an individual without intellectual stability whose sallies sometimes hit the mark and sometimes miss (Pope's **wit** invariably hits its target). Only the last of these, contrasting 'trips a lady' with 'struts a lord', is strictly a full antithesis with a strong opposition. Yet there is still an opposition between the apparently innocuous trifling fop (when he is at the dressing table in the company of women) and the more sinister corrupted flatterer (dining with men). The antithesis is brilliantly sustained and extended within the phrase 'Amphibious thing', for Sporus can operate successfully in two elements, the male and female spheres, and by implication has the attributes of both sexes. This might in other contexts be a virtue, but here serves further to muddy the waters with suggestions of a dishonourable sexual ambiguity that picks up earlier hints in the phrases 'master up' and 'miss' that are further pursued in the rest of the portrait.

In a second example, the balanced antithetical structure is varied by the use of another figure, the **chiasmus**, a figure of arrangement in which the word order of one phrase or clause is reversed in the next. The poet is pointing here to the fate that awaits society ladies in their old age if they live solely by the values of polite society, 'the world':

> See how the world its veterans rewards!
> A youth of frolics, an old age of cards;
> Fair to no purpose, artful to no end,
> Young without lovers, old without a friend;
> A fop their passion, but their prize a sot,
> Alive, ridiculous, and dead, forgot!
> (*Epistle to a Lady*, lines 243–8)

The strong pattern of dismissive antitheses, emphasised by the regularity of the break in the middle line in the second, third, fourth and fifth lines, is suddenly varied in the second half of the fifth line by the positioning of the word 'sot', a drunkard, at the end. Had the previous pattern continued the order would have been 'but a sot their prize'. The reversal gives the 'sot' pride of place and puts him in opposition to 'a fop' at the beginning (the fop has presumably turned into a sot). The variation is a slight surprise, giving great emphasis to the rhyme word and so preparing for the final clinching dismissal in 'forgot'.

A condensed antithesis of a kind highly congenial to Pope's cast of mind is the **oxymoron**, a figure which unites in close juxtaposition ideas that seem sharply contradictory, as in the following example which turns on the difference between true and false learning: 'The bookful blockhead, ignorantly read, / With loads of learned lumber in his head (*An Essay on Criticism*, lines 612–3).

In more general ways Pope's wit revels in **paradox** and inversion:

A *little learning* is a dangerous thing;
Drink deep, or taste not the Pierian spring:
There shallow draughts intoxicate the brain,
And drinking largely sobers us again.
(*An Essay on Criticism*, lines 215–8)

The basic meaning is simple enough; read widely in poetry (drink deeply from the Muses' spring) to acquire the necessary experience on which to base critical judgements which otherwise may be the result of rash enthusiasm. The success and surprise of these lines stems from the poet's witty extension of the metaphor of drinking for reading into the paradoxical expression of the last two lines where the couplet arrangement brings out the contrast not only within each line but also between the two lines.

In this example from *An Essay on Criticism* Pope is arguing a point. His poetry, generally speaking, has a strong argumentative structure, something it inherits from the poetry of the Renaissance and which it shares with the poetic output of the period in general. Its clarity in this respect led the influential critic T.S. Eliot (1888–1965) to call the poetry of the age of Dryden and Pope 'the poetry of statement'. Whatever Eliot meant to convey by this infelicitous phrase, it has encouraged the view that what Pope writes can best be described as little more than versified prose. It is certainly true that, unlike modern poetry (especially poetry like that of Eliot himself), it has the virtues of prose, in that connections are supplied and the syntax is clear. But even when Pope is arguing in verse, there is a strong metaphorical element which may be exemplified in the opening of his philosophical poem *An Essay on Man*:

> Awake my St JOHN! Leave all meaner things
> To low ambition and the pride of kings.
> Let us (since life can little more supply
> Than just to look about us and to die)
> Expatiate free o'er all this scene of man;
> A mighty maze! but not without a plan:
> A wild, where weeds and flow'rs promiscuous shoot;
> Or garden, tempting with forbidden fruit.
> Together let us beat this ample field,
> Try what the open, what the covert yield!
> The latent tracks, the giddy heights, explore
> Of all who blindly creep, or sightless soar;
> Eye Nature's walks, shoot folly as it flies,
> And catch the manners living as they rise;
> Laugh where we must, be candid where we can;
> But vindicate the ways of God to man.
> (Epistle I, lines 1–16)

Pope is addressing Lord Bolingbroke, the guide, philosopher and friend, who had encouraged him in this literary enterprise, and is inviting him (and through him, the reader of his poem) to accompany him in a literary and philosophic enterprise in which he will 'vindicate the ways of God to man'. This philosophic enterprise is likened to an exciting day out in the country where away from 'meaner things' they (and we) can 'Expatiate free o'er all this scene of man'. The scene of man is variously figured as a 'maze', a 'wild' and a 'garden', which in their various contradictory associations of the hidden plan, beauty amidst disorder, and tempting fruit even where nature is dressed to advantage in the garden, suggest complexity, variety and paradox. In its literal meaning 'expatiate' is ' to walk about at large, to wander at will'; as a metaphor, it is 'to speak or write at some length'. In a philosophic poem the metaphorical meaning is the primary one but the poet makes a play with the literal meaning of the word by extending the idea it sets in train, and by metaphor represents the philosophic enterprise not simply as a desultory country walk but as a purposeful day out on the grouse moor where they are to bag game. Beating the field, seeing what the covert yields, exploring hidden tracks and giddy heights, eyeing 'Nature's walks', shooting folly and catching the manners living as they rise, all these expressions are connected to the central figure of the game-shoot. The imagery is highly appropriate in that, while it may be doubted whether shooting was one of Pope's pastimes, it certainly was the kind of aristocratic pursuit that could be associated with his noble friend; the greater appropriateness is to the nature of Pope's literary enterprise itself, for the imagery suggests that there will be thorough exploration and dismissal of erroneous views, that Nature (in the sense illuminated above) will be the ground of the work, that folly will be ridiculed and that the poet will convincingly represent human characteristics and behaviour in the universal light of nature. This opening shows that the language of this philosophical poem will be largely metaphorical. (It also shows that Pope moulded his closed couplets seamlessly into paragraphs; the paragraph is the basic unit not the individual couplet.) The wit that makes the relation between the basic philosophic or literary enterprise and the physical imagery, in the first instance, suggests freedom, since the scene of man is variously figured, but also suggests purpose when it comes to the extended metaphor of the game-shoot (a kind of conceit). The result is an utterance that is imaginatively subtle, that suggests more than it states and that is, therefore, far removed from prose statement.

It is an utterance too that exemplifies well what Pope has to say about witty imagery in *An Essay on Criticism*:

> Some to *conceit* alone their taste confine,
> And glittering thoughts struck out at every line;
> Pleased with a work where nothing's just or fit;
> One glaring chaos and wild heap of wit.
> (*An Essay on Criticism*, lines 289–92)

He does not actually denigrate 'conceit' altogether here, only an excess of it in works where it is not appropriately applied and controlled as it is, for example, in the opening of *An Essay on Man*.

Rhetorical devices in

Figures abound in *The Rape of the Lock*, ably exploited for comic effect. In the following example, there are a number of features in the arrangement of the language that contribute to the overall effect.

> Not youthful kings in battle seized alive,
> Not scornful virgins who their charms survive,
> Not ardent lovers robbed of all their bliss,
> Not ancient ladies when refused a kiss,
> Not tyrants fierce that unrepenting die,
> Not Cynthia when her manteau's pinned awry,
> E'er felt such rage, resentment, and despair,
> As thou, sad virgin! for thy ravished hair! (Canto IV, lines 3–10)

Most obviously the repetition of the first word 'not' (called **anaphora**) gives emphasis and pattern. Since the sense is not completed until the final couplet, the syntax is suspended over six lines, creating a build-up of suspense until it is eventually concluded in the climax of the final couplet. Although the pauses are at different points in the first six lines, there is obviously a regular pattern in their rhythm and movement which is quite disturbed in the concluding couplet, with emphatic pauses after the three nouns delineating Belinda's emotions before the climax, intensified by the direct address to Belinda, and by the **antithesis** in 'virgin' and 'ravished'. The rhetorical climax, though, also wittily proves to be an anticlimax, for the final word 'hair', skilfully paired with its rhyme word 'despair', weighs very lightly; when all is said and done, the ravished virgin has only lost her hair! What proves to be an imbalance between the penultimate and the final line has been well prepared for in the pattern of the **similes** in the previous six lines. In each case a serious simile, featuring 'youthful kings', 'ardent lovers' and 'tyrants fierce', is succeeded by an example of wilful female petulance in the 'scornful virgins' 'ancient ladies' and 'Cynthia when her manteau's pinned awry'. The juxtaposition, which makes brilliant use of the form of the closed couplet, in which one line can be balanced against another, is mainly humorous but also has the effect, through the accumulation of examples, of associating Belinda with the unpleasant female petulance that has gone before. The comic imbalance between the lines comes to suggest a larger imbalance in

Belinda's reaction and indeed in the female society to which she is implicitly compared. The 'rage, resentment, and despair' are belittled by the rhetorical context in which they occur. There is judgement as well as comedy in these lines.

Pope exploits incongruity not only between lines but also within lines:

> Or stain her honour, or her new brocade;
>
> Forget her prayers, or miss a masquerade;
>
> Or lose her heart, or necklace, at a ball;
>
> Or whether Heaven has doomed that Shock must fall. (Canto II, lines 107–10)

The moral 'honour', spiritual 'prayers' and emotional 'heart' are balanced against the physical and material here. The serious and the less serious are comically joined. This joining is wittily expressed through another rhetorical figure, the **zeugma** (from the Greek, meaning 'yoking'). The syntax yokes together two different meanings of the words 'lose' and 'stain', uniting the literal and the metaphorical. In both cases the literal meaning belongs to the glittering world of polite society, which is implicitly put into perspective by the zeugma, which unites it with something more serious. The rhetorical figure of the zeugma could be said to express in miniature the larger design of the poem; in *The Rape of the Lock*, the trivial and the serious are conjoined (perhaps in the very title itself) not merely for comic effect but so that a serious perspective is brought to bear upon the triviality of the beau monde in general and of the characters of the poem in particular, who have allowed a trivial incident to be blown out of all proportion.

The zeugma is a most effective deflationary tool:

> Here Britain's statesmen oft the fall foredoom
>
> Of foreign tyrants, and of nymphs at home;
>
> Here thou, great ANNA! Whom three realms obey,
>
> Dost sometimes counsel take – and sometimes tea. (Canto III, lines 5–8)

The zeugma uniting two different kinds of fall initiates a fall from the dignified, which is comically extended in a second zeugma in which the Queen takes counsel and tea. A few lines later, the dignity of proceedings at Hampton Court has descended further with 'singing, laughing, ogling, and all that' (line 18).

RHETORICAL DEVICES IN THE RAPE OF THE LOCK continued

Almost anywhere in the poem, it is possible to see that the couplet arrangement is being exploited to aid the sense. At the critical moment, as so often in literature, things come in threes when the sylphs try to warn Belinda of the approaching Baron: 'And thrice they twitched the diamond in her ear; / Thrice she looked back, and thrice the foe drew near' (Canto III, lines 137–8). The neat syntactical arrangement whereby three sentences each containing the word 'thrice' are contained within the couplet mimics the action in its rhetorical structure.

Other rhetorical devices are used incongruously for comic effect. The **apostrophe** (literally, turning away), when the poet breaks away from his narrative role directly to address a character or to offer a sententious reflection to the reader, is used comically in the card game when the king of clubs falls victim to the queen of trumps.

> What boots the regal circle on his head,
> His giant limbs, in state unwieldy spread;
> That long behind he trails his pompous robe,
> And, of all monarchs, only grasps the globe? (Canto III, lines 71–4)

The rhetorical question (a question that does not require an answer because the answer is obviously implied by the form in which the question is put) is purely comic here where it is posed about a playing card. When later after the game has ended, the poet turns to make a moral point with a sententious exclamation on Belinda's triumph, the effect is more serio-comic.

> Oh thoughtless mortals! ever blind to fate,
> Too soon dejected, and too soon elate.
> Sudden, these honours shall be snatched away,
> And cursed for ever this victorious day. (Canto III, lines 101–5)

There is a kind of truth here. The comedy comes largely through the exaggerated language; 'honours' and 'victorious day' have an **ironic** ring when applied to winning a hand of cards.

Hyperbole, exaggerated language, is basic to the poem, occurring throughout. Particularly comic examples are in the elation of Belinda after victory in the card game followed by horror after the cutting of the lock.

The nymph exulting fills with shouts the sky;
The walls, the woods, and long canals reply! (Canto III, lines 99–100)

Then flashed the living lightning from her eyes
And screams of horror rend th' affrighted skies. (Canto III, lines 155–6)

We may well feel that Belinda has a right to be annoyed, but the exaggerated expression has the comic and deflationary effect of reducing her reactions to absurdity.

A figure that aids this linguistic enlargement is **periphrasis**, or talking round a thing rather than directly addressing it. The pair of scissors with which the lock is cut in Canto III is never directly called a pair of scissors but is first a 'two edged weapon' (line 128), then more daringly 'The little engine' (line 132) and finally, in the grandest periphrasis, at the climactic moment as the Baron actually uses it, it becomes 'the glittering forfex' (line 147). When coffee is taken, the delight of those enjoying the repast is reflected in the delight that the periphrastic language communicates to the reader, as the coffee is heated on lacquered furniture and pored into China cups.

On shining altars of Japan they raise
The silver lamp; the fiery spirits blaze:
From silver spouts the grateful liquors glide,
While China's earth receives the smoking tide; (Canto III, lines 107–10)

There may be satire in the use of 'altars', implying that the taking of coffee is treated with a seriousness more appropriate to religious ritual, but the periphrastic language has an exotic, imaginative appeal, making something beautiful and grand out of the commonplace and familiar.

PART FOUR

EXTENDED COMMENTARIES

TEXT 1   THE RAPE OF THE LOCK (CANTO V, LINES 7–66)

Then grave Clarissa graceful waved her fan;
Silence ensued, and thus the nymph began:
   'Say, why are beauties praised and honoured most,
The wise man's passion, and the vain man's toast?   10
Why decked with all that land and sea afford?
Why angels called, and angel-like adored?
Why round our coaches crowd the white-gloved beaux?
Why bows the side-box from its inmost rows?
How vain are all these glories, all our pains,   15
Unless good sense preserve what beauty gains;
That men may say, when we the front-box grace,
Behold the first in virtue as in face!
Oh! if to dance all night, and dress all day,
Charmed the smallpox, or chased old age away;   20
Who would not scorn what housewife's cares produce,
Or who would learn one earthly thing of use?
To patch, nay ogle, might become a saint,
Nor could it sure be such a sin to paint.
But since, alas! frail beauty must decay,   25
Curled or uncurled, since locks will turn to grey;
Since painted, or not painted, all shall fade,
And she who scorns a man, must die a maid;
What then remains but well our power to use,
And keep good-humour still whate'er we lose?   30
And trust me, dear! good-humour can prevail,
When airs, and flights, and screams, and scolding fail.
Beauties in vain their pretty eyes may roll;
Charms strike the sight, but merit wins the soul.'
   So spoke the dame, but no applause ensued;   35
Belinda frowned, Thalestris called her prude.
'To arms, to arms!' the fierce virago cries,

And swift as lightning to the combat flies.
All side in parties, and begin th' attack:
Fans clap, silks rustle, and tough whalebones crack;   40
Heroes' and heroines' shouts confusedly rise,
And bass and treble voices strike the skies.
No common weapons in their hands are found,
Like gods they fight, nor dread a mortal wound.
   So when bold Homer makes the gods engage,   45
And heavenly breasts with human passions rage;
'Gainst Pallas, Mars; Latona, Hermes arms;
And all Olympus rings with loud alarms;
Jove's thunder roars, heaven trembles all around,
Blue Neptune storms, the bellowing deeps resound: 50
Earth shakes her nodding towers, the ground gives way,
And the pale ghosts start at the flash of day!
   Triumphant Umbriel on a sconce's height
Clapped his glad wings, and sate to view the fight:
Propped on their bodkin spears, the sprites survey   55
The growing combat, or assist the fray.
   While through the press enraged Thalestris flies,
And scatters deaths around from both her eyes,
A beau and witling perished in the throng,
One died in metaphor, and one in song.   60
'O cruel nymph! a living death I bear,'
Cried Dapperwit, and sunk beside his chair.
A mournful glance Sir Fopling upwards cast,
'Those eyes are made so killing' – was his last.
Thus on Maeander's flowery margin lies   65
Th' expiring swan, and as he sings he dies.

The Baron has cut the lock. First Sir Plume and then Belinda herself have appealed to him to restore it, but in vain. At this point, Clarissa suggests a different tactic. Her speech was added to the poem in 1717 in response to criticism that the poem lacked a moral. It has sometimes been argued that the speech is improper in her mouth because she had earlier assisted the Baron in providing him with the scissors and is thus an accomplice in the rape. On the other hand, it could be argued that this gives her special authority to say what she says, as she treats the cutting of the lock for the trivial incident it is. But as we are not privy to her motives, who can say? It is certainly significant that it comes from one of the characters within the social world of the poem (rather than from the narrator's voice) and that that character is a woman. The late addition of the speech may go some way to accounting for its general reflective nature (indeed Clarissa's name might suggest a general clarifying role), for it seems as much to address the overall position of the 'belles' in this society as respond to the demands of this particular moment in the plot of the poem.

Clarissa's appeal to the virtues of good sense and good humour puts the whole world of *The Rape of the Lock* into perspective as well as the cutting of the lock of hair that took place within it. She speaks from within as one of the beauties of this world referring to 'our coaches', 'all our pains'; like Belinda she too puts on her make-up to be admired and enter the fray. Beauty is power in this world but the only way to preserve that power when beauty yields to time is to maintain 'good sense' which will command respect.

'What then remains, but well our power to use, / And keep good-humour still, whate'er we lose?' There is an appeal here to the highest form of self-interest and in the line 'And she who scorns a man, must die a maid' a warning of the dire consequences of female petulance. The unmarried state in the early eighteenth century held no possibilities for women. It is not that Clarissa is urging Belinda to yield to the Baron, nor is it to be supposed that she is urging good humour in the event that a woman suffers a real loss of honour. The reference to loss surely puts a perspective on the triviality of what has been lost in the poem. Good humour is the means by which a woman might exercise her power rather in the manner of the addressee in the later *An Epistle to a Lady* (Martha Blount, the embodiment of good sense and good humour in the poem), when she 'Charms by accepting, by submitting sways, / And has her humour most when she obeys' (lines 263–4). So there is a certain realism and worldly wisdom in the advice of Clarissa, given by one coquette to another. In the immediate action of the poem, Clarissa is suggesting that Belinda gives up hysterics and tries a good-humoured approach which will have more chance of a happier outcome for herself.

Many of Pope's more learned readers must have recognised in Clarissa's speech an allusion to a famous speech in Homer's *Iliad*,

which had already been published in translation by Pope, in which
the Trojan hero Sarpedon lays bare the motivation of the aristocratic
warrior and defines the heroic impulse that urges him to join the
fight:

>Resolved alike, divine Sarpedon glows
>With generous rage that drives him on the foes.
>He views the towers, and meditates their fall,
>To sure destruction dooms the aspiring wall;
>Then casting on his friend an ardent look,
>Fired with the thirst of glory, thus he spoke:
> 'Why boast we, Glaucus! Our extended reign,
>Where Xanthus' streams enrich the Lycian plain,
>Our numerous herds that range the fruitful field,
>And hills where vines their purple harvest yield,
>Our foaming bowls with purer nectar crowned,
>Our feasts enhanced with music's sprightly sound?
>Why on these shores are we with joy surveyed,
>Admired as heroes, and as gods obeyed,
>Unless great acts superior merit prove,
>And vindicate the bounteous powers above?
>'Tis ours the dignity they give to grace;
>The first in valour, as the first in place;
>That when with wondering eyes our martial bands
>Behold our deeds transcending our commands,
>Such, they may cry, deserve the sovereign state,
>Whom those that envy dare not imitate!
>Could all our care elude the gloomy grave,
>Which claims no less the fearful than the brave,
>For lust of fame I should not vainly dare
>In fighting fields, nor urge thy soul to war.
>But since, alas! ignoble age must come,
>Disease, and death's inexorable doom;
>The life, which others pay, let us bestow,
>And give to fame what we to nature owe;
>Brave though we fall, and honoured if we live,
>Or let us glory gain, or glory give!'

> He said; his words the listening chief inspire
> With equal warmth, and rouse the warrior's fire;
> The troops pursue their leaders with delight,
> Rush to the foe, and claim the promised fight.
> (*Iliad*, XII, lines 365–400)

Death and disease afflict the polite and the heroic world alike (the Baron had died of smallpox in 1713 after the first edition of the poem in 1712). The miniaturisation of the epic original has a comic effect (Homer is indeed **parodied**) but recognition of the source actually intensifies the seriousness of the parody. Pope's **wit** has found occult resemblances between things apparently unlike: the heroic warrior culture of ancient Greece, and the feminised drawing-room world of the beau monde.

The battle of the belles and beaux that ensues, after Clarissa's advice falls on deaf ears, is purely comic. Its style achieves the same high pitch that we find illustrated in the extract from the Homer translation; the comedy arises from the incongruous content that inhabits the style – clapping fans, rustling silks and tough whalebones that crack. But when Pope comes to the **simile** 'So when bold Homer', the narrative in itself is entirely serious and differs little from its source:

> Such war the immortals wage; such horrors rend
> The world's vast conclave, when the gods contend.
> First silver-shafted Phoebus took the plain
> Against blue Neptune, monarch of the main:
> The god of arms his giant bulk displayed
> Opposed to Pallas, war's triumphant maid.
> (*Iliad*, XX, lines 91–6; in Pope's version)

What is comic is the incongruous application of the simile. From the grand gods of Homer with their earth-shattering power that throws the whole creation into turmoil, we come now to their miniature counterparts in the little world of the polite society as Umbriel and his sprites, like the Homeric gods (but also unlike them) survey the mortal fight below. One of the sources of the poem's fascination and appeal stems from this constant shifting in perspective and tone.

The actual battle is partly physical but mostly **metaphorical**. Thalestris kills figuratively with her looks. Dapperwit, whose name suggests neatness of wit, dies 'in metaphor' saying that he bears 'a living death'; Sir Fopling dies in song, quoting from an opera 'Those eyes are made so killing'. It is an ingeniously fitting stroke of wit on the poet's part to illustrate these figurative deaths figuratively. The final simile figuring the dying swan is in itself a moment of beauty that is by no means nullified by the comic incongruity of its context.

TEXT 2 EPISTLE TO MISS BLOUNT, ON HER LEAVING THE TOWN AFTER THE CORONATION

As some fond virgin, whom her mother's care
Drags from the town to wholesome country air,
Just when she learns to roll a melting eye,
And hear a spark, yet think no danger nigh;
From the dear man unwilling she must sever, 5
Yet takes one kiss before she parts for ever:
Thus from the world fair Zephalinda flew,
Saw others happy, and with sighs withdrew;
Not that their pleasures caused her discontent,
She sighed not that They stayed, but that She went. 10
    She went to plain-work, and to purling brooks,
Old-fashioned halls, dull aunts, and croaking rooks:
She went from opera, park, assembly, play,
To morning-walks, and prayers three hours a-day;
To part her time 'twixt reading and bohea, 15
To muse, and spill her solitary tea,
Or o'er cold coffee trifle with the spoon,
Count the slow clock, and dine exact at noon;
Divert her eyes with pictures in the fire,
Hum half a tune, tell stories to the squire; 20
Up to her godly garret after seven,
There starve and pray, for that's the way to heaven.
    Some squire, perhaps, you take delight to rack;
Whose game is whisk, whose treat a toast in sack;
Who visits with a gun, presents you birds, 25
Then gives a smacking buss, and cries, – 'No words!'

Or with his hound comes hallowing from the stable,
Makes love with nods, and knees beneath a table;
Whose laughs are hearty, though his jests are coarse,
And loves you best of all things – but his horse.   30
　　In some fair evening, on your elbow laid,
You dream of triumphs in the rural shade;
In pensive thought recall the fancied scene,
See coronations rise on every green;
Before you pass th' imaginary sights   35
Of lords, and earls, and dukes, and gartered knights,
While the spread fan o'ershades your closing eyes;
Then give one flirt, and all the vision flies.
Thus vanish sceptres, coronets, and balls,
And leave you in lone woods, or empty walls!   40
　　So when your slave, at some dear idle time,
(Not plagued with head-aches, or the want of rhyme)
Stands in the streets, abstracted from the crew,
And while he seems to study, thinks of you;
Just when his fancy points your sprightly eyes,   45
Or sees the blush of soft Parthenia rise,
Gay pats my shoulder, and you vanish quite,
Streets, chairs, and coxcombs rush upon my sight;
Vexed to be still in town, I knit my brow,
Look sour, and hum a tune, as you may now.   50

Zephalinda, a name (from the Greek zephyr) that suggests a delicate spring breeze, finds herself removed from her natural habitat in the fashionable town to an altogether unwelcome environment in the country, where manners (social habits) are unsophisticated and old fashioned. The poet imagines her boredom being only partially relieved by flirtations with the local booby squire. He imagines her caught up in the fancy that she can see in the country the recent glittering scenes she has witnessed at the coronation, until she is awakened from this reverie by a sudden movement made by her fan and she is left feeling more alone in this place which is empty of excitement. The poet sympathises with her as he imagines himself in a similar predicament, when amid the vexations of the town, there rises in his mind a vision of Zephalinda herself which is just as easily dispatched when some friend pats him on the shoulder. He then feels acutely the irritations of the town just as she might feel those of the country.

The opening **simile**, which in its imagery helps to define the social world to which Zephalinda belongs, is artful in evoking a situation which may or may not be that of Zephalinda herself. In the simile the mother removes her daughter just when she is learning the arts of courtship but before she is aware of any lurking danger from the fashionable young man, the 'spark', with whom she is flirting. The exaggerated melodrama of her emotional parting is emphasised in the **feminine rhyme** of 'sever' with 'for ever' (see Techniques, on Refinement of the Heroic Couplet). The young girl in the simile is slightly mocked but, although Zephalinda is associated with her, the association is not direct, so that if there is mockery it is not at Zephalinda's expense. In what follows, too, Zephalinda is absolved of any bad feeling, for with great precision the poet makes the reason for her discontent absolutely clear. This clarity is emphatically rendered in the rhyme of 'discontent' with 'went'. The downright finality of her discontent and its cause are conveyed by the rhythm of the final deliberately prosaic monosyllabic line. The last word, emphasising her leaving the town which is the subject of the poem's title, is duly emphatic and picked up in the next paragraph: 'She went to plain-work'; the style at this point is fittingly plain. But this deliberate plainness is immediately enlivened by a stroke of **wit**. The 'plain-work' refers to one of the few occupations available to Zephalinda in the country, needlework, and is playfully paired with 'purling brooks' (bubbling streams), a stale poetical cliché enlivened by the pun in 'purling', a kind of stitch, more complicated than the simpler 'plain-work' practised in the country. There is comedy in the close juxtaposition of 'dull aunts' and 'croaking rooks', with its comic suggestion of croaking aunts. The comedy is continued in the next couplet which juxtaposes the pleasures and entertainments of fashionable London with bracing walks and long sessions of prayer. The lines that follow evoke a life of boredom and rigid routine. London society dines in the late afternoon and entertainment continues well into the evening. Zephalinda eats early and has to go to her 'godly garret' after seven o'clock. This is a life of self-denial, whose rewards are not in the present: 'There starve and pray, for that's the way to heaven'. The tone here is **ironic**; after what has gone before, it is clear not only that we are being invited to see things from Zephalinda's point of view, but that the values of this life are not being endorsed.

In the interlude with the hearty country squire, the comedy intensifies. His lack of sophistication is indicated in the game he plays, 'whisk' (ombre is the fashionable game in *The Rape of the Lock*), and 'sack' that he drinks, which is the drink of the labouring classes. To pay a visit was one of the elegant rituals of aristocratic life, a formality arranged through the medium of servants who would deliver visiting cards announcing the social intentions of their masters and mistresses. The squire has come straight from the stable with his gun after a game-shoot in violation of all the rules of upper-class etiquette. The dead birds are an indelicate gift for a fashionable lady and might with more propriety have been given to the cook. The 'smacking buss' is another such violation of etiquette. Fashionable manners might allow a polite kissing of the lady's hand, but certainly not a 'buss', the character of which may be guessed at from the following quotation given in the *OED*: 'we buss our wantons, but our wives we kiss'. The noisy physicality of the squire, well suggested in his 'smacking buss', is extended further when he is envisaged as coming from his natural habitat, the stable, 'hallowing' (an onomatopoeic word) with his hound. His courting methods are crude like his jokes. The joke against him is delightfully delivered in the final line which reveals his true love and the extent of his gallantry. Once again the key features of the squire and his world are emphasised in the rhyme words 'coarse' and 'horse'.

In its next movement, the tone changes as the poet imagines Zephalinda's daydreaming. The daydream does not simply consist of the memory of the recent coronation but an imaginative transformation of her present situation when the countryside, 'the rural shade', is obliterated by 'coronations' rising 'on every green'. The stately rhythm of the line listing the dukes and earls, through its monosyllables and the simple device of the repetition of 'and', in its movement vividly underscores the imagined procession. The imagination and Zephalinda's total absorption in it are given free rein until the sudden movement of the fan brings her back from her 'vision' to a lonely and empty reality. The sharp contrast between the two last lines of the final couplet makes the abruptness of the change from illusion to reality dramatically emphatic.

In its last movement, the poem takes a surprising turn as the poet, in the town, takes upon himself the role of gallant, calling himself Zephalinda's 'slave' and imagines himself caught up in a similar reverie at an idle moment (wittily made memorable by the **oxymoron** in 'dear idle') in which he daydreams about Zephalinda, until this is dispelled by a tap on his shoulder resulting in a return to an unwelcome reality. In quite different circumstances he is similarly vexed. As Zephalinda had hummed a tune, so does he. The knitting of his brow might facetiously correspond to her needlework. The correspondences may be thought to mask differences in value: for Zephalinda the town is a place of glamour, for the poet it is congested and full of fools. But Pope's wit finds and lays stress upon hidden resemblances between situations and, we may believe, people that are 'apparently unlike', to coin a phrase of Johnson's. It is this uniting of disparate elements that gives the poem its artful conclusion and underlying coherence.

In sum, this poem is clear and precise in its expression and imagery. It delivers itself easily in crisp couplets. It combines the detachment of wit, humour and a developed ironical sense with psychological insight and imaginative sympathy. It is worldly, urbane and good humoured. If Zephalinda read it, she can only have been charmed by the compliment it contains.

TEXT 3   AN EPISTLE TO A LADY (LINES 24–25)

But what are these to great Atossa's mind?	115
Scarce once herself, by turns all womankind!	
Who, with herself, or others, from her birth	
Finds all her life one warfare upon earth:	
Shines, in exposing knaves, and painting fools,	
Yet is, whate'er she hates and ridicules.	120
No thought advances, but her eddy brain	
Whisks it about, and down it goes again.	
Full sixty years the world has been her trade,	
The wisest fool much time has ever made.	
From loveless youth to unrespected age,	125
No passion gratified except her rage,	

So much the fury still outran the wit,
The pleasure missed her, and the scandal hit.
Who breaks with her, provokes revenge from hell,
But he's a bolder man who dares be well.   130
Her every turn with violence pursued,
No more a storm her hate than gratitude:
To that each passion turns, or soon or late;
Love, if it makes her yield, must make her hate:
Superiors? death! and equals? what a curse!   135
But an inferior not dependant? worse!
Offend her, and she knows not to forgive;
Oblige her, and she'll hate you while you live:
But die, and she'll adore you – Then the bust
And temple rise – then fall again to dust.   140
Last night, her lord was all that's good and great;
A knave this morning, and his will a cheat.
Strange! by the means defeated of the ends,
By spirit robbed of power, by warmth of friends,
By wealth of followers! without one distress,   145
Sick of herself through very selfishness!
Atossa, cursed with every granted prayer,
Childless with all her children, wants an heir.
To heirs unknown descends th' unguarded store,
Or wanders, heaven-directed, to the poor.   150
   Pictures like these, dear Madam, to design,
Asks no firm hand, and no unerring line;
Some wandering touches, some reflected light,
Some flying stroke alone can hit 'em right:
For how should equal colours do the knack?   155
Chameleons who can paint in white and black?
   'Yet Cloe sure was formed without a spot' –
Nature in her then erred not, but forgot.
'With every pleasing, every prudent part,
Say, what can Cloe want?' – She wants a heart.   160
She speaks, behaves, and acts, just as she ought;
But never, never reached one generous thought.
Virtue she finds too painful an endeavour,

Content to dwell in decencies for ever.
So very reasonable, so unmoved, 165
As never yet to love, or to be loved.
She, while her lover pants upon her breast,
Can mark the figures on an Indian chest;
And when she sees her friend in deep despair,
Observes how much a chintz exceeds mohair! 170
Forbid it heaven, a favour or a debt
She e'er should cancel – but she may forget.
Safe is your secret still in Cloe's ear;
But none of Cloe's shall you ever hear.
Of all her dears she never slandered one, 175
But cares not if a thousand are undone.
Would Cloe know if you're alive or dead?
She bids her footman put it in her head.
Cloe is prudent – Would you too be wise?
Then never break your heart when Cloe dies.

Nearly halfway through the **satire** comes its most extended portrait which is generally held to refer to Catherine Sheffield, Duchess of Buckinghamshire, the illegitimate daughter of James II. It follows a series of lesser examples of female inconsistency, instability and error ('these' in the opening line) and proves in its length and complexity to be the centrepiece of the epistle.

Atossa was an historical personage, the daughter of a Persian king. The name also suggests the Greek word for whirlwind. This is one of the ideas that gives the portrait its unity; she is by 'turns' all womankind, her life is 'warfare', her 'eddy brain / Whisks' thought about, she is a 'fury' ('Her every turn with violence pursued'), with both her hatred and her gratitude being a 'storm' to which 'each passion turns'. Through this she emerges as an unstable and extreme character of violent shifts and radical inconsistencies.

All her virtues are turned into vices, and these turns are made emphatic and striking by the **rhetorical** arrangement within the lines of the couplet. Although she has **wit** and can expose fools, she is 'whate'er she hates and ridicules'. The second line undercuts the first. Her worldly wisdom and experience are acknowledged but turned to ridicule by the combination of an **oxymoron** and contradiction in the second undercutting line of the couplet: 'The wisest fool much time has ever made'. The couplet structure encourages the occurrence of an **antithetical** reply in a second line to a thesis proposed in the first. There are strong antitheses throughout: 'loveless youth' and 'unrespected age', 'passion' and 'rage', 'fury' and 'wit', 'pleasure' and 'scandal', 'love' and 'hate', 'offend' and 'oblige', 'last night' and 'this morning' and so on. Their occurrence is varied sufficiently to prevent the portrait becoming too formulaic or schematic. With 'superiors', 'equals' and 'inferiors' the doubling pattern is varied with a tripartite arrangement which occurs in a different way spread over three couplets beginning with 'offend', 'oblige' and 'die'.

As the poet reflects on the strangeness of her character towards the end, Atossa ceases to be merely ridiculous and elicits sympathy. Her goals – power, friends, followers – are not revealed to be shallow or misguided. She is defeated in the means by which she pursues those ends, by an excess of things which in themselves are desirable: spirit, warmth and wealth. She is the victim of her own excess and, unlike Sporus (see Techniques, on Rhetorical Features) she has the self-knowledge to be 'sick of herself'. With all her material wants supplied in abundance, she is pitifully 'cursed with every granted prayer', not necessarily having prayed for the wrong things. She outlives all her children, and is powerless to project her will and influence on to the next generation but paradoxically her fortune benefits the poor. The satire here elicits pathos as we are made to reflect on a cruelly wasted talent and energy. Pope's portraits are chilling because, although we know that satire exaggerates, we can see writ large through the distorted lens all the follies, absurdities, vanities, inconsistencies and self-deceptions that are necessarily attendant upon the human condition.

At this point, the poet comments on his own pictures as he addresses the good lady to whom he is writing the epistle. His remarks are of great interest because the analogy with the art of painting enables him to suggest that his pictures are not simply black and white but subtly shaded to capture the chameleon (the changeable) in human nature.

His addressee then puts forward the character of Cloe as an example to set against this catalogue of contradiction and inconsistency. Cloe is indeed the perfect society lady 'formed without a spot', the perfect product of upper-class social formation in her age, but 'Nature in her then erred not, but forgot'. The dialogue between the poet and the interjecting addressee continues: ' "With every pleasing, every prudent part, / Say what can Cloe want?" – She wants a heart.'

In this portrait is explicitly played out a more general conflict that underlies Pope's satire, the opposition between the social being and the spontaneous natural self. The two voices continue as the poet takes over from the addressee. Here is the voice supporting the thesis that Cloe is virtuous:

> She speaks, behaves, and acts just as she ought …
> So very reasonable, so unmoved …
> Observes how much a chintz exceeds mohair!
> Forbid it, heaven, a favour or a debt
> She e'er should cancel …
> Safe is your secret still in Cloe's ear
> Of all her dears she never slandered one …
> Cloe is prudent

There is quite a catalogue of virtue here, in fact all the virtues conventionally associated with high society in the eighteenth century; prudence, decorum, propriety, reasonableness, unflappable calm, discriminating taste, discretion, control, dignity – but in the brilliant dialectic of the couplet the antithetical reply insisting that her virtue is a denial of nature turns all her qualities negatively into the essential limitation of mere social form. This portrait of an elegant society lady in her world of chintz, a footman and an Indian chest, is itself elegant and polished and as such embodies the virtues of the age in which it was painted. But elegance and polish are not enough. The values of the age are turned against it. The moral point made through and controlling the wit in this instance could not be clearer: social living like art itself must reflect the universal light of Nature.

PART FIVE

Background

Pope's life & literary career

Alexander Pope, born in 1688, the only son of moderately well-to-do Catholic parents (his father was a linen merchant), had a London childhood in comfortable circumstances. When still a boy, he contracted a form of tuberculosis which resulted in curvature of the spine and stunted growth; when adult, he was only four foot six tall. His condition worsened with age, leading him to talk of 'this long disease, my life' (*Epistle to Dr Arbuthnot*, line 132). It entailed physical pain and some dependence upon others, making any kind of active career in the political, social or commercial world virtually impossible. His opportunities were further restricted by his parents' religion. Catholics were forbidden entry into university, so that he never had the formal university education that his abilities deserved. His family moved to the Berkshire village of Binfield situated within the royal forest of Windsor when he was about twelve. He was educated partly by priests at home, then subsequently under the tutelage of a former fellow of University College Oxford who had set up a school near Marylebone.

His talent for and dedication to poetry were evident at a very early age. He says himself, 'As yet a child, nor yet a fool to fame / I lisped in numbers [verse], for the numbers came' (*Epistle to Dr Arbuthnot*, lines 127–8). He began by consciously imitating the style of admired English predecessors and by making translations of short extracts from the Greek and Roman classics. His first major work was a series of four *Pastorals* evoking the four seasons in sweetly harmonious verse, published when he was only twenty-one in 1709. This was followed in 1711 by *An Essay on Criticism*, an exuberantly witty verse epistle in which he sought to clarify for himself and his times both the principles necessary for the formation of good judgement and the spirit in which the critic should set about his task. In the course of it he renews, in contemporary terms, traditional ideas about art and its relation to the nature of things that were part of the common European inheritance from the classical world (see Literary Background). Here is the most attractive and positive representation of that broad-based humanism, in the light of which he would attack false learning, improper study, short views, narrow interests and bad taste in his later **satires** and **moral essays**. *Windsor Forest*, begun earlier but published in 1713, celebrates the history of the forest and the cultivated harmony of its landscape, a harmony secured by the recent Peace of Utrecht, allowing the poet to envisage a new Golden Age:

> Here Ceres' gifts in waving prospect stand,
> And nodding tempt the joyful reaper's hand;
> Rich Industry sits smiling on the plains,
> And peace and plenty tell a STUART reigns.
>
> ...
>
> Fair Liberty, Britannia's Goddess, rears
> Her cheerful head, and leads the golden years. (lines 39–42 and 91–2)

His first publications in the years 1709–13, including the first edition of *The Rape of the Lock* (1712) which was immediately popular, brought him instant fame and success. In this period he made a number of enduring friendships with leading literary figures like the satirist Jonathan Swift (1667–1745), John Gay (1685–1732), author of *The Beggar's Opera*, Thomas Parnell (1679–1718), a minor poet who later gave him scholarly help in his epic translations, Dr John Arbuthnot (1667–1735), man of letters and the Queen's physician and a leading Tory politician, the Earl of Oxford. Together they were members of an association calling itself the 'Scriblerus Club' designed in Pope's words to his friend Joseph Spence (*Anecdotes ... of Books and Men*) to ridicule 'all the false tastes in learning under the character of a man [Martinus Scriblerus] that dipped into every art and science but injudiciously in each'. The group ceased to meet formally after the death of Queen Anne in 1714.

The year 1714 was a momentous one in the life of Pope, for on 23 March he signed a contract with the publisher Bernard Lintot for the translation in six volumes of the *Iliad* of the Greek epic poet Homer. The project was financed by subscriptions, on the proceeds of which Pope gained financial independence and security, and the freedom to pursue a literary career independent of patronage. As he later put it himself, '(thanks to Homer) since I live and thrive, / Indebted to no Prince or Peer alive' (*The Second Epistle of the Second Book of Horace*, lines 68–9). The final volume of the *Iliad* came out in 1720, after which he went on to translate the *Odyssey*.

Although the Homer translation was the main preoccupation of his literary life for more than a decade, he continued with other projects, publishing *Eloisa to Abelard*, for example, in 1717. When he came to publish his *Works* in 1717, therefore, he had produced a great variety of poems in widely different genres.

As a result of his literary earnings, a year after his father died he moved into an elegant country house (no longer surviving – except for Pope's grotto) at Twickenham in 1718, then well outside the city of London, where he lived with his mother until her death in 1733 and then on his own (for he never married) until his own death in 1744.

At Twickenham, Pope was able to lead the settled and prosperous life of an eighteenth-century gentleman and to indulge his passion for garden design. He championed a new informality (see *An Epistle to Richard Boyle, Earl of Burlington*), eschewing the more formal designs of the French which had never been greatly popular in England. Of his life at Twickenham, Dr Johnson writes in his *Life of Pope*:

> Here he planted the vines and the quincunx [a rectangular arrangement of five trees with one in the middle] which his verses mention; and being under the necessity of making a subterranean passage to a garden on the other side of the road, he adorned it with fossil bodies, and dignified it with the title of a grotto; a place of silence and retreat, from which he endeavoured to persuade his friends and himself that cares and passions could be excluded.

He cultivated his garden with diligence and, detached at Twickenham from the life of business and the court, yet near enough the centre to be in touch, he lived out his version of the good life, dedicated to friendship, conversation and books, that is recommended in many of his poems, notably the verse epistles and of those particularly *The Imitations of Horace*. A collection of letters in prose extending to four large volumes, some of which he published in his own lifetime, adds to the poetic record in documenting the style and values of the man and of his various interests and social relationships. Although he could be waspish and was not a man to cross, he had a genuine talent and need for friendship that extended from a circle of like-minded intellectuals of both sexes to the companionship of a succession of much loved Great Danes.

After he had translated Homer, Pope, who had in Johnson's description a mind 'active, ambitious and adventurous, always investigating always aspiring', conceived the ambitious plan of writing 'a system of ethics in the Horatian way', of which *An Essay on Man* completed in 1734 and *The Moral Essays* (of which *An Epistle to a Lady* published in 1735 was one) were to be a part. He gave up the grand plan, but his output in poetry was now almost exclusively devoted to the didactic, the moral and the satiric, as he seems to acknowledge himself when reviewing his career in *An Epistle to Dr Arbuthnot*: 'be one poet's praise … That not on fancy's maze he wandered long / But stooped to truth, and moralized his song' (lines 340–1). Fancy here perhaps refers to purely imaginative poems like the *Pastorals* or *Eloisa to Abelard*.

Although Pope's poetry had made him famous, it had also attracted a great deal of adverse critical comment, much of which was the product of envy and malice that was also intermingled with vicious personal attacks. His adversaries readily seized upon his physical weakness and deformity, and much play was made with the letters of his name A. P…E. John Dennis (1657–1734), for example, a leading critic of the day, in an attack upon *An Essay on Criticism* (1711), abused him in the following terms.

> Let the person of a gentleman of his parts be never so contemptible, his inward man is ten times more ridiculous; it being impossible that his outward form, though it be that of a downright monkey, should differ so much from human shape as his unthinking immaterial part does from human understanding.

In *An Epistle to Dr Arbuthnot*, he refers to 'The libelled person, and the pictured shape' (line 353). As early as 1717, in the preface to his *Works*, he remarked that 'the life of a wit is a warfare on earth'. And that warfare was conducted in the early eighteenth century with a quite shocking ferocity. Though he had the support of friends, he was always a controversial figure in the life of his times. Even the Homer translation involved him in controversy when he quarrelled with another leading critic, the more genial figure of Joseph Addison (1672–1719), over the latter's promotion of a rival (and inferior) version of the first book of the *Iliad* published by his protégé, Thomas Tickell (1686–1740). Addison's verdict, which has been contradicted by every subsequent critic who has looked into the matter, was that both were good but that Tickell's had more of Homer in it. Pope's private response was to compose the portrait of 'Atticus', the false critic, later included in *An Epistle to Dr Arbuthnot* (lines 193–214).

He did not intend publication at the time but the portrait circulated among his friends, one of whom, Francis Atterbury, the Bishop of Rochester, encouraged him to employ further the talent that it showed for sharp satire. But it was not until Lewis Theobald (1688–1744), in his edition of Shakespeare of 1726, pointed to the deficiencies of Pope's own edition of Shakespeare published in the previous year, that Pope, possibly to forestall further criticism, entered the warfare of the wits with a vengeance that delighted his supporters and dismayed his enemies. *The Dunciad*, a satirical poem attacking the mediocrity and venality of the whole literary world of the day, with Theobald as its hero, was published anonymously in 1728, though Pope's authorship was immediately suspected. The poem, like Swift's *Gulliver's Travels* (1726), doubtless owed much to this early association of the leading wits of the age in the Scriblerus club. Thereafter, he was drawn increasingly to controversial satire in a moral crusade against iniquitous tendencies in the cultural life of his times. *An Epistle to Dr Arbuthnot* (1735) offers a personal defence of this poetic crusade, which is foreshadowed in *An Essay on Criticism*, but to which he first harnessed his satirical talents in *The Dunciad*. In his last years his major project was a series of *Imitations of Horace* begun in 1733 and ending in 1738, through which he was able to continue his moral and satirical crusade by adapting the persona of a great classical predecessor, who was also a satirist and moralist, to the particular circumstances of his own life and times. This was followed by a major revision of *The Dunciad*, adding an apocalyptic fourth book in 1742 and bringing the poem up to date with a new hero, the poet laureate Colley Cibber in 1743.

As a professional man of letters who was concerned with his own fame and whose work was sought after and read even by those who disliked him, he was much preoccupied throughout his literary career with the task of revising poems for subsequent editions and updating collections of his works. He was working on a final edition of his poems in the last months of his life. It is reported that, three weeks before he died, he was sorting out presentation copies of the first volume of this edition for his friends with the comment, 'Here am I, like Socrates, distributing my morality among my friends just as I am dying'. He died peacefully at Twickenham surrounded by friends on 30 May 1744. Subsequent volumes of the edition of his works were produced by his literary executor, William Warburton. In his will he left property to a life-long friend Martha Blount to whom he had earlier dedicated literary epistles and who was the addressee of *An Epistle to a Lady* in 1735, whose praises he had sung at the end of the poem.

Historical background

At the time, and more so in retrospect, the year of Pope's birth was a momentous one in British constitutional history. For the second time in the century an English monarch was deposed. The execution of Charles I in 1649 came after a prolonged civil war and resulted in the rule of Oliver Cromwell, followed by the restoration of the Stuart monarchy in 1660. It must have seemed to those who opposed the absolutism of Charles I that little had been gained after two decades of upheaval, for, although Charles II was invited back by Parliament with whom he negotiated terms, the powers of the monarchy were little restricted. Charles II ruled with greater sensitivity than his father, but the Stuart monarchy came to grief over a question that proved beyond his powers to solve. Charles himself had no legitimate children so that his natural heir on the hereditary principle was his younger brother, the Catholic James, Duke of York. The religion of James was seen to be a threat to the established church and to the traditional independence of Britain. Forces in Parliament, predominantly Dissenters (Protestants who separated themselves from the communion of the established church of England) and low Anglicans proposed to exclude James from the throne. They were opposed by the king and those supporting the royal prerogative who were generally high Anglicans. It was at this time that the terms Whig and Tory were first used in opposition, as abusive terms to describe supporters and opponents of the Exclusion Bill. To some extent, this polarisation echoed the religious and political polarisation of the earlier civil war. The king and the anti-exclusionists prevailed, and James succeeded on Charles's death in 1685. His conduct as king, however, confirmed the fears of his opponents and alarmed many of his supporters, who felt that the established constitution of church and state was in danger.

Whigs and Tories joined forces in 1688 to invite over the Dutch Prince William of Orange, husband of James's daughter Mary, who had been brought up on the instructions of Charles II in the Protestant faith. James's army deserted in large numbers and he took refuge in Catholic France at the court of Louis XIV, who continued to uphold his claim to the throne. Parliament offered the throne jointly to William and Mary on conditions set out in a Bill of Rights. The hereditary principle was replaced by a parliamentary succession and the sovereign was required to be Protestant. A number of provisions in the bill shifted power away from the monarch and towards Parliament. Thenceforward the government of the kingdom was more of a partnership between the monarch and the Parliament largely controlled by the nobility. The absolutist tendencies of the Stuart monarchs before 1688 were checked and thereafter England had a more mixed constitution, in marked contrast to the absolute monarchy holding sway in France. Nevertheless, the monarch continued to exercise great power, and the royal prerogative in appointments and dismissals remained effective throughout the eighteenth century. The Toleration Act of 1689 allowed freedom of worship for Dissenters (though not for Catholics) so that in the so-called 'Glorious Revolution' of 1688–9 a constitutional settlement was achieved without bloodshed that was broadly acceptable to a majority in the kingdom.

Supporters of the exiled James, known as Jacobites from the Latin version of his name Jacobus, were thereafter always a small minority including many Roman Catholics, some Tory Anglicans who questioned the legitimacy of the succession in 1688, and later, largely for dynastic reasons, many Scots, for the house of Stuart had formerly ruled in Scotland, before the union of crowns after the death of Elizabeth I in 1603, when James VI of Scotland became James I of England.

As Catholics, Pope's family might have felt excluded from the settlement of 1689, for Catholics experienced a variety of restrictions relating to property and residence, education, politics and professional life. Technically they were required to live ten miles from the centre of London. The universities were not open to them, nor could they hold public office. Nevertheless, their minority status did not hinder their economic activity, even though they were subject to special taxes. Pope's father was a successful businessman. The poet himself retained the religion of his upbringing. In his letters and his poems his Catholicism is not much in evidence, and it is apparent that his religious beliefs were tolerant and enlightened. Nonetheless, his religion must have set him apart to some extent from the mainstream of English life. In practice, there was increasing toleration of Catholics doctrinally and at the same time continuing suspicion of them politically, in view of the perceived threat from the king over the water. In 1689 James landed in Ireland and was defeated by William at the Battle of the Boyne. In 1708 there was an abortive French invasion. In 1715 came the first Jacobite uprising in Scotland in support of James's son James Edward, whose claim was recognised by the king of France and who was known subsequently as the Old Pretender, and in the year after Pope died, came the final uprising in 1745 in favour of Charles Edward, grandson of James II and called the Young Pretender.

When Pope began his literary career, the childless William and Mary had been succeeded by Mary's younger sister Anne. England was heavily involved in foreign campaigns prosecuted by the Duke of Marlborough, who had succeeded William III as leader of the grand alliance of English and Dutch forces against the power of France. Party rivalry in this period was intense and centred upon Tory resistance to religious toleration promoted by the Whigs and upon Tory attempts to bring an end to the long foreign campaign, which was a drain on the resources of the gentry. Whig views on foreign policy were promoted by Joseph Addison in *The Spectator* and by Richard Steele in *The Tatler*. The Tory view was promoted in pamphlet form by Jonathan Swift. The Tories were in power when the Peace of Utrecht celebrated in *Windsor Forest* was signed in 1713. Tories and Whigs were not formally organised into parties and the terms are only loosely connected with easily defined values and interests. In this period, the Tories are usually identified with the established Anglican church and the squirearchy, and the Whigs with the interests of Dissenters, the landowning aristocracy and the commercial interests of the rising middle classes.

An issue that divided Whigs and some Tories concerned the succession to Queen Anne, none of whose offspring had survived childhood. Even before she came to the throne, Parliament had decreed in 1701 that the succession should go to her nearest Protestant relative,

Sophia, the Electress of Hanover, the granddaughter of James I. The Tories re-opened the issue in the last year of her reign when illness made her demise likely, making overtures to James Edward, the son of James II, which foundered when he refused to give up his Catholicism. Nevertheless, when the queen died, the Tory cause was greatly damaged. The new King George, the son of Sophia who had just predeceased Anne, naturally chose his ministers from the Whigs, who had staunchly supported the Hanoverian accession, and who would remain in the ascendancy for the next fifty years. Many Tories had supported the Hanoverian accession, but they were seriously weakened by association with their Jacobite brethren, particularly in the wake of the Jacobite uprising in Scotland in 1715.

The Whig ministry was soon dominated by the personality and policy of Sir Robert Walpole, who held the offices of First Lord of the Treasury and Chancellor of the Exchequer continuously from 1721 to 1742. He aimed through continuing Whig supremacy to secure the Hanoverian succession against any aspirations to the contrary among Tory Jacobites. The twin pillars of the policy by which he gained several election victories were economic success with low taxation and a peaceful foreign policy. He gained the confidence of George I (1714–27) and of his son who succeeded him, and was able to use their power of royal patronage to party advantage. Never before had so much power been concentrated in any of the monarch's ministers, and this great power itself was often the main target of attack on the part of his critics. To opponents his extensive network of patronage was corrupt, and his peaceful foreign policy an expediency which appeased Britain's commercial rivals. The unpopularity of individual financial measures could be exploited by the opposition, but in general Walpole's economic management was successful. Many historians look back upon his rule as a time of political stability and growing national prosperity.

Pope had always had social contacts across the main religious and political divisions, though his own inclinations were undoubtedly Tory, as his early association with the Scriblerians might indicate. To what extent he may from time to time have had Jacobite leanings, it is difficult to say. In *Windsor Forest* he happily identified himself with the ruling powers in the land and praised the peace of Utrecht, recently negotiated by the Tories and disapproved of by many Whigs. After 1714, he was no longer a political 'insider', but since as a Catholic he was not eligible for office, he could never have contemplated the kind of career in which literature went hand in hand with government service, as in the case of the Whig Addison or the Tory Swift. Hence the events of 1714 were not the personal blow to Pope that they were to his Protestant friend Swift. In an age when most literary men had some clear political affiliation and when poets were courted by politicians, perhaps because of his religion and his health, Pope remained more detached than most. In this he was aided by the financial independence he achieved through his Homer translation. He was never a party man and never addressed political issues as directly as, for example, John Dryden, who as poet laureate at the court of Charles II had written many poems in support of the government, notably *Absalom and Achitophel* in 1686. Pope always prided himself upon his independence, and in his poems his expression is often teasingly elusive:

> My head and heart thus flowing through my quill,
>
> Verse-man or prose-man, term me which you will,
>
> Papist or Protestant, or both between,
>
> Like good Erasmus, in an honest mean,
>
> In moderation placing all my glory,
>
> While Tories call me Whig, and Whigs a Tory.
>
> (*The First Satire of the Second Book of Horace Imitated*, lines 63–8)

Nevertheless part of that independence was not merely detachment but conscious opposition to Walpole and all his works. *The Imitations of Horace* are not exclusively political poems, but one of the more marked ways in which they differ from their originals, in which the Roman poet Horace represents himself as a friend of Augustus and in broad sympathy with the ruling order, stems from Pope's oppositional stance.

LITERARY BACKGROUND

Pope is regarded as one of the chief exponents of **Neoclassicism** and the greatest poet of the **Augustan** age of English literature. It is the function of this section to clarify the meaning of these concepts insofar as they can be applied to his poetry.

NEOCLASSICISM

The cry 'imitate the ancients' was heard long before the age of Pope. It goes back, in fact, to the humanists of the early Renaissance. The Renaissance literally suggests rebirth, a rebirth of an interest in antiquity; the humanists of the Renaissance were those who desired through the study of 'litterae humaniores', ancient literature, history and philosophy, to pattern their thinking on ancient lines. In the artistic sphere this fostered the impulse to recreate ancient forms in all areas of the arts and put them to modern uses. It should be stressed that at its creative best this impulse did not aim at the simple reproduction of the ancients (such an aim where it existed was a snare and a delusion since the world had moved on from antiquity), but rather sought inspiration from the great ancients as a spur to fresh creative endeavour in the present. This impulse to refer back to classical models intensified in seventeenth-century France and in the period of maximum French influence in England, from 1660 when Charles II, who in the company of leading royalists had spent his exile at the French court, was restored to the British throne.

The best introduction to Pope's Neoclassicism is to be found in one of his earliest works, *An Essay on Criticism* of 1711. In this verse epistle, loosely modelled on *The Art of Poetry* by the Roman poet Horace, he sought to clarify for himself and his times both the principles necessary for the formation of good judgement and the spirit in which the critic should set about his task. In the course of this, he renews in contemporary terms traditional **humanist** ideas about art and its relation to the nature of things that were part of the common European inheritance from the classical world. The *Essay* is also the most positive and attractive representation of that broad-based humanism, in the light of which he would attack false learning, improper study, short views, narrow interests and bad taste, in his later moral essays and **satires**.

To set the poem in its context, the *Essay* was written at a time when the so-called 'Querelle des anciens et des modernes', which had caused much intellectual ferment in France, was reverberating in Britain. One extreme felt that the moderns could not possibly compete with the established masterpieces of the ancients – modern culture was inevitably overshadowed; the other that the unenlightened ancients had been superseded by the moderns writing in an age when man had come of age through the exploration of the natural sciences. In the *Essay* Pope avoids extremes and is neither ancient nor modern. The comprehensiveness of his mind precluded allegiance to the narrower dogmas of his day:

> Some foreign writers, some our own despise;
> The Ancients only, or the Moderns prize.
> Thus wit, like faith, by each man is applied
> To one small sect, and all are damned beside.
> …
> Regard not then if wit be old or new,
> But blame the false, and value still the true. (lines 394–7, 406–7)

The central proposition in which the broad-based humanism of the *Essay* is grounded is a declaration of faith, almost a hymn to the divine and unchanging light of nature, in language that suggests the first cause:

> First follow *Nature*, and your judgment frame
> By her just standard, which is still the same:
> Unerring NATURE, still divinely bright,
> One clear, unchanged, and universal light,
> Life, force, and beauty, must to all impart,
> At once the source, and end, and test of art. (lines 68–73)

Here is Pope's belief in the underlying order that gives dignity, beauty and meaning to the cosmos. Included in this metaphysical conception is a statement about the nature of man. Within the grand scheme of things, human beings have their appointed place, and stand in the same relation to nature, irrespective of considerations of time and place, or culture and society.

The proposition put forward in the *Essay*, 'Nature and Homer were, he found, the same' (line 135), entails a belief, widely held in the era of Neoclassicism, that, however different archaic Greece and modern Britain might be, these differences are the accidents of time and place, for what Homer has achieved in his poems is the representation of humanity in its timeless aspects. Homer enables us to see how human beings stand in relation to nature, to things as they are.

The equation of Homer with nature may be said to embrace both content and form; what is natural is both the object represented, that is, human passions and actions, and the manner of its representation, that is, narrative method and style. Let us take, for example, the main plot of the *Iliad*, revolving around the anger of Achilles. Insulted by Agamemnon, the leader of the Greeks, at the beginning of the poem, he withdraws from the fighting; even when the Greeks are in dire straits because most of their principal fighters have been wounded, he persists in his anger and cannot be persuaded to return, but he does relent to the extent of allowing his friend Patroclus to fight in his stead, wearing his armour. When Patroclus is killed by the Trojan Hector, who mistakes him for Achilles, he is distraught with grief and guilt and returns to the fighting for vengeance. He kills Hector and then dishonours his corpse: heroic achievement and human glory for which he has sacrificed his life (he was given a choice: everlasting fame and early death, or a long undistinguished life) now mean nothing to him. The poem ends, after he has finally relented of his anger and agreed to a ransom for the body of Hector, with a lament for the lot of men who are the victims of an arbitrary fate.

Homer does not waste time telling us about inessential aspects of Achilles' life and character that do not have a bearing upon his anger, nor does he tell us about the siege of Troy from the beginning. He begins in the middle of things, concentrating attention only upon those particulars which relate to his central theme. This selectivity. Homer's *method*, enables us to see Achilles' behaviour in a clear light, because we are given a central core without distracting and inessential particulars. Of course, much of the *Iliad* may seem to have little direct bearing upon the main action, but in the final analysis the episodes are subordinate to the irreducible plot. Achilles is powerfully individualised so that it is not being suggested that Pope has created bloodless archetypes. But he has arranged his main plot around the anger of Achilles in such a way as to give us a pattern of behaviour that, in its causes and effects, represents a probable if not inevitable sequence. Underneath all that is particular and individual, the anger is typical in its causes and consequences, and it is Homer's method that enables us to see this. Homer, the first artist of the Western tradition (from about the eighth century BC), has therefore accomplished in his poems all that Aristotle the philosopher and critic later held to be the end of art; he has imposed form and order on the undifferentiated matter and random chaos of life, thus enabling us to see through the particular to the universal.

The central proposition about nature is immediately followed in the *Essay* by an injunction to the would-be critic to have due regard for the **rules** of art. A preoccupation with the rules of art is an ancient one and not merely an aberration of this particular period. In other arts it is perhaps easier to understand the emphasis upon basic ground-rules of the craft. In antiquity the ideal proportion between height and breadth in a building or between limbs and torso in the representation of the human form was arrived at in the first place by precise measurement. In the Renaissance great artists like Leonardo da Vinci (1452–1519) and Albrecht Dürer (1471–1528) made mathematical studies of proportion and consciously set out to establish rules that constituted their findings. The rules are not regarded as a human invention, but exist, and are given in the nature of things, rather as the laws of physics describe the underlying pattern of the natural world: 'Those RULES of old discovered, not devised, / Are Nature still, but Nature methodized' (lines 88–9).

The discovery of the rules is particularly associated with the name of Aristotle whose *Poetics*, a fragmentary work emanating from the late fourth century BC in Greece, is mostly about tragedy but has incidental remarks about epic and other **genres**. Aristotle identifies the object and end of tragedy, and breaks the form into its constituent parts, analysing the means by which the end is achieved in the best sort of tragedy. He therefore himself bequeathed a method which, by the time of Pope, had been systematically extended by Italian and French critics to other classical genres such as comedy or pastoral, and even to nonclassical genres such as tragicomedy or romance. Rules might concern the use of particular metres for particular genres, the need to keep the genres distinct and separate, to adopt an appropriate style (grand for epic or humble for pastoral), to observe proportion in structure (five acts for drama), to observe the three unities in drama, to keep consistency in characterisation, and to use spectacle and divine intervention sparingly, rigorously to subordinate the parts to the whole, thereby keeping the end in view all the time, and so on. At root of all this, of course, is the Renaissance admiration for the classics of Greece and Rome, which were thought to have established standards of excellence in the various genres. These inspired literary masterpieces are seen to embody principles of organisation and design, which had enabled the poet to render the truth of things in the most appropriate form: 'Learn

hence for ancient rules a just esteem; / To copy nature is to copy them'
(lines 139–40).

The just esteem for ancient rules felt by Pope is balanced in the
Essay by a vigorous defence of the poet's right boldly to deviate from the
common track and essentially to make his own rules, for rules are but a
means to an end and there is a grace beyond the reach of art:

> If, where the rules not far enough extend,
>
> (Since rules were made but to promote their end)
>
> Some lucky licence answers to the full
>
> Th' intent proposed, that licence is a rule.
>
> Thus Pegasus, a nearer way to take,
>
> May boldly deviate from the common track.
>
> Great wits sometimes may gloriously offend,
>
> And rise to faults true critics dare not mend;
>
> From vulgar bounds with brave disorder part,
>
> And snatch a grace beyond the reach of art,
>
> Which without passing through the judgement, gains
>
> The heart, and all its end at once attains. (lines 146–57)

Pegasus, the winged horse of Greek myth and here a figure for the poet
in imaginative flight, is not to be reined in by too much rigid control. On
the other hand, ancient rules deserve respect. There is here a typical
Popean balance between the demands of the traditional inheritance for
restraint and the need of the creative artist for individual liberty.

THE AUGUSTAN AGE

This term has both a political and an artistic dimension, for the
understanding of which it is necessary to have some knowledge of the
period in Roman history which gives it its name.

As a period term in Roman civilisation it covers the rule of Rome's
first emperor from the time when, after he had defeated Mark Antony at
the battle of Actium in 31BC, he renounced the power he had held as the
triumvir Octavian and adopted the name Augustus from 27BC to his
death in AD14. Abroad Augustus consolidated the conquests of his
predecessors by a programme of urbanisation and a series of treaties with
neighbouring states by which he secured the Roman frontiers; at home he

revised the old Republican constitution, investing supreme power in himself as imperator, commander of the armed forces, though disguising his power under republican forms, for his rule was ratified annually by the Senate and the popular assembly. After nearly a century of wars and civil strife, including two major civil wars, he gradually brought peace, order and stability to Rome and her dominions. He initiated moral reforms in which he attempted to breathe new life into the old religion and instituted a grand programme of public building, so that it was said of him that he found Rome brick and left it marble. He fostered the arts through the patronage of his friend Maecenas. The foremost poets of the age, Virgil and Horace, though they had been on the opposing side in the civil war, accepted the patronage of Maecenas, identified themselves with the new order, and gave expression in their poems to the new mood of self-confidence generated by the **Augustan** peace. Their poems are sometimes called Augustan to denote their relation to the political order and to suggest the conditions under which they were produced. This may be said to be the political meaning of Augustan as applied to literary works of the period.

The term, however, goes further than this to suggest a quality in the art of the poems, for the works of Virgil and Horace have been seen to have a formal polish and a refinement of expression that set them apart from the literature of the previous age, and a poise and balance that set them apart from the literature that followed. These qualities of polish, refinement, urbanity and poise have been considered to be the hallmarks of Augustan literature, representing the high-water mark of Roman culture and civilisation. It is the indubitable fact of the supreme literary achievement of Virgil and Horace that has sustained and propagated an Augustan myth wherein Latin comes to perfection of expression in the golden age of the rule of Augustus (the phrase 'golden Latin' being a commonplace of Roman literary history), made possible by the interlocking relationship of poetry, patronage and political power, for Virgil and Horace achieve greatness not in spite of Augustus but because of him.

This myth, embodying an ideal for some, masking reality for others, exerted a powerful fascination upon the nation states of modern Europe, seeking in their cultural aspirations to emulate Greece and Rome. Many Renaissance poets wrote poems heralding their princes and patrons in the

name of Augustus or Maecenas. In Britain John Dryden, in his poem
Astraea Redux, celebrates the restoration of the British monarchy in 1660
and indirectly heralds Charles II as a new Augustus:

> O happy age! O times like those alone
> By fate reserved for great Augustus' throne!
> When the joint growth of arms and arts foreshew
> The world a monarch, and that monarch you. (lines 318–21)

The poet uses the reign of Augustus as the ideal pattern of imperial and
cultural greatness (the one being consequent upon the other) to prophecy
a similar growth in national greatness for the British state. Literary
historians have indeed applied the term Augustan broadly to refer to the
period from 1660 to about 1780 or sometimes more narrowly to
coincide more or less with the age of Pope, that is starting with the reign
of Queen Anne in 1701 and continuing through to the mid eighteenth
century.

The youthful Pope in the reign of Queen Anne had celebrated
the peace of Utrecht (which brought peace between Britain and France)
in *Windsor Forest*, a poem inspired by the *Georgics* in which Virgil
had celebrated man's fruitful cultivation of the natural world in the
Italian countryside, made possible after peace had been restored to the
political order by Augustus: 'Rich Industry sits smiling on the plains, /
And peace and plenty tell, a STUART reigns' (lines 41–2). But after
the Stuart dynasty came to an end with the death of Queen Anne in 1714
and a change of political leadership from Tory to Whig, Pope no
longer identified himself with the ruling powers in the land, becoming
with the passing of time increasingly alienated from the government
and its aims. Furthermore the financial independence he gained
from the Homer translation allowed him to be free of patronage and
the court. In his imitation of the verse epistle addressed by Horace
to Augustus (with whom the Roman poet is said to have had cordial
relations), he brilliantly uses the Augustan parallel for satirical effect,
since the Hanoverian King George Augustus (his actual name) to
whom he addresses Horace's lines, in the power of Whig politicians
and no lover of poetry (in his reign Colley Cibber, later to be hero of
Pope's new *Dunciad*, was created poet laureate), was no Caesar and no
Augustus:

> While you, great Patron of Mankind! sustain
>
> The balanc'd World, and open all the Main;
>
> Your Country, chief, in Arms abroad defend,
>
> At home, with Morals, Arts, and Laws amend;
>
> How shall the Muse from such a Monarch steal
>
> An hour, and not defraud the Public Weal?
>
> (*The First Epistle of the Second Book of Horace Imitated*, lines 1–6)

Although his relation to the Horatian original is **ironic** at the opening here and at the end where he again addresses the august majesty of the king, in the main body of the epistle he is concerned with two arguments that seek to set a value upon poetry and to vindicate the literature of his time.

The first concerns the role of poetry in the *civitas*; in its highest form poetry is useful to the state, *utilis urbi*: 'Yet let me show, a Poet's of some weight, / And (tho' no Soldier) useful to the State' (lines 203–4). The argument continues by asserting that the great **genres** like epic and drama in which the Greeks excelled have a moral civilising function. There is no doubt that Pope strongly identified with Horace, in their common endeavour in the humbler genre of the **moral essay** to fulfil the civilising office of the poet as the standard-bearer and guardian of cultural values.

The second thrust of the epistle is the vindication of the Augustan aesthetic (and moral) values of refinement, urbanity and polish:

> Wit grew polite, and Numbers learn'd to flow.
>
> Waller was smooth; but Dryden taught to join
>
> The varying verse, the full-resounding line,
>
> The long majestic March, and Energy divine.
>
> Tho' still some traces of our rustic vein
>
> And splay-foot verse, remain'd, and will remain.
>
> Late, very late, correctness grew our care,
>
> When the tir'd Nation breath'd from civil war. (lines 266–73)

Pope regarded Waller as an early exponent of refinement in the use of the closed couplet (see Techniques, on Refinement of the Heroic Couplet), though of his predecessors Dryden is here celebrated as the greatest exponent of metrical virtuosity in the couplet, for simple refinement is not enough. Dryden's genius was to energise the newly refined medium.

'**Correctness**', artistic refinement and polish, the aspiration of the age endorsed here by Pope and supremely embodied in his own literary output, is at the same time reckoned to be a poor thing on its own. In the *Essay on Criticism*, the poet warns the critic not to make a fetish of it:

> Survey the Whole, nor seek slight faults to find
> Where nature moves, and rapture warms the mind;
> Nor lose, for that malignant dull delight,
> The generous pleasure to be charmed with wit.
> But in such lays as neither ebb, nor flow,
> Correctly cold, and regularly low,
> That shunning faults, one quiet tenor keep;
> We cannot blame indeed – but we may sleep. (lines 235–42)

PART SIX

CRITICAL HISTORY & FURTHER READING

EARLY RESPONSES

Pope's poetry occasioned much debate and controversy from the beginning. He was attacked on personal, moral, religious and poetical grounds (see Background, on Life & Literary Career). Recently a scholar of the period has collected more than 100 pamphlet attacks published in the poet's lifetime. In the preface to his *Works* of 1717, he declared that 'the life of a wit is a warfare on earth'. That warfare was conducted with great ferocity, and Pope was much provoked before he entered it decisively himself with the first edition of *The Dunciad* in 1728. Thereafter he constantly felt the need to defend his personal and poetical integrity. The reception of his poetry among his contemporaries determined to some extent the direction his career took in its second half.

The first major critical assessment of his poetry came not long after his death with the publication by Joseph Warton (1722–1800), himself a poet, of *An Essay on the Writings and Genius of Pope*, the first volume of which came out in 1756, treating the early poetry up to and including *Eloisa to Abelard*. In the dedicatory letter he questioned whether there was anything very sublime or pathetic in the poetry of Pope and, in his summing up, he predicted that Pope's reputation would rest on poems like *Eloisa*, because contemporary **satire** is rendered obsolete by time: 'For **wit** and satire are transitory and perishable, but nature and passion are eternal.' In the second volume published in 1782, he sums up as follows:

> It will appear that the largest portion of them is of the didactic, moral and satiric kind; and consequently, not of the most poetic species of poetry; whence it is manifest that good sense and judgement were his characteristical excellencies, rather than fancy [imagination] and invention; not that the author of the *Rape of the Lock* and *Eloisa* can be thought to want imagination, but because imagination was not his predominant talent, because he indulged it not and because he gave not so many proofs of this talent as of the other ... Whatever poetical enthusiasm

> he actually possessed, he withheld and stifled. … Surely it is no narrow and
> niggardly encomium to say he is the great poet of reason, the first of ethical
> authors in verse.

To some extent Warton is reflecting the beginnings of a change of taste
and sensibility away from **Neoclassicism** that was taking place in the mid
eighteenth century, but the questions he first raised: Can there be a
hierarchy of subjects and kinds? Did Pope suppress his imaginative
side? Did he make an inferior choice in concentrating upon the moral,
the didactic and the satiric? Is satire a lower and transient form? – these
questions have been much debated and raise in their turn fundamental
questions about the nature of poetry itself.

In his *Life of Pope* (1781), one of the most trenchant, judicious and
challenging accounts of the poet, Samuel Johnson (1709–84), probably
with the verdict of Warton in mind, takes a different view:

> Pope had, in proportions very nicely adjusted to each other, all the qualities that
> constitute genius. He had *Invention*, by which new trains of events are formed, and
> new scenes of imagery displayed, as in *The Rape of the Lock*, and by which extrinsic
> and adventitious embellishments are connected to a known subject, as in the *Essay
> on Criticism*. He had *Imagination*, which strongly impresses on the writer's mind,
> and enables him to convey to the reader, the various forms of nature, incidents of
> life, and energies of passion, as in his *Eloisa*, *Windsor Forest* and *Ethic Epistles*. He
> had *Judgement* which selects from life or nature what the present purpose requires,
> and by separating the essence of things from its concomitants, often makes the
> representation more powerful than the reality: and he had *colours of language* always
> before him, ready to decorate his matter with every grace of elegant expression, as
> when he accommodates his diction to the wonderful multiplicity of Homer's
> sentiments and descriptions.

> After all this, it is surely superfluous to answer the question that has once been
> asked, Whether Pope was a poet? Otherwise than by asking in return, If Pope be
> not a poet, where is poetry to be found? To circumscribe poetry by a definition will
> show only the narrowness of the definer, though a definition that shall exclude
> Pope will not easily be found.

For Johnson, the poetry of Dryden and Pope represented a peak of
achievement in English literature, while Warton looked back to the
Elizabethan age, in particular to the poetry of William Shakespeare and

Edmund Spenser, and in his own times to the poetry of Thomas Gray (1716–71) for what he called poetry that was truly pathetic and sublime.

In the **Romantic** era (traditionally regarded as beginning with the poetry of William Wordsworth and Samuel Coleridge just after the French Revolution in 1789), there was continued controversy about the status and character of Pope's poetic achievement. As *the* great poet of the previous century, modern poets could not ignore him and his poetry proved the battleground over which contemporary debates about taste raged in what is sometimes called 'the Pope controversy'. Those who depreciated Pope did so chiefly on two grounds. The first related to his subject matter and extended the criticism of Warton, that it was essentially 'unpoetic' because it dealt with the artificial manners of a high society which was itself perhaps under threat after the revolution in France and which was no longer considered to be the primary focus of the poet's attention. Modern poets turned away from the social world to external nature and to those simple and elemental passions which were felt to reside in those who lived closest to nature. This is the view famously propounded by Wordsworth in his preface to *Lyrical Ballads* (1800). Wordsworth and Coleridge also attacked Pope on the grounds of his expression, particularly in relation to his translation of Homer. Warton, in saying that there was nothing sublime or pathetic in Pope (a verdict that must have surprised many his contemporaries who admired the Homer translations), ignored the translation of Homer on the grounds that it was not original. For Johnson, on the other hand, 'that poetical wonder, the translation of the *Iliad*', was a national treasure and at the centre of his poetical achievement; he devotes more attention to it in his *Life* than to any other work. Wordsworth and Coleridge, however, used Pope's Homer as their chief target when they launched their attack on what they called the poetic diction or sometimes the pseudo-poetic diction of the previous century. For them it was a prime example of the kind of artificiality in expression from which as modern poets writing in a different idiom they wished to break away.

Not all the Romantics, however, turned their back on Pope. An interesting case is that of Lord Byron, an archetypal Romantic poet, who nevertheless exhibited in his satires and verse epistles a more traditional **Augustan** side and was an ardent champion of Pope. He was one of the few Romantics who could write good **heroic couplets** himself; he looked back to Pope as one of his poetic mentors, genuinely appreciating his **wit**, his hatred of cant and his verbal dexterity. In an age when humour was not much in evidence in modern productions, despite his own tendency to gloomy misanthropy, he shared with Pope an impish sense of humour. He even defended passages attacked by Coleridge from the Homer translation. As to subject matter, he issued this rejoinder to those like Warton who depreciated the kinds of poetry in which Pope excelled: 'There may or may not be, in fact, different "orders" of poetry, but a poet is always judged according to his execution, not according to the branch of his art.'

A typical Romantic attitude is exhibited by the critic William Hazlitt who calls Dryden and Pope 'the great masters of the artificial style of poetry in our language', where the assumption is that this is a lesser kind, but goes on to offer a finely tuned appreciation of *The Rape of the Lock*:

> It is the most exquisite specimen of *filigree* work ever invented. It is admirable in its proportion as it is made of nothing. … It is made of gauze and silver spangles. The most glittering is given to everything, to paste, pomatum, billet-doux, and patches. Airs, languid airs, breathe around – the atmosphere is perfumed with affectation. A toilette is described with the solemnity of an altar raised to the Goddess of vanity, and the history of a silver bodkin is given with all the pomp of heraldry. No pains are spared, no profusion of ornament, no splendour of poetic diction, to set off the meanest things. The balance between the concealed irony and the assumed gravity is as nicely trimmed as the balance of power in Europe. The little is made great, and the great little. You hardly know whether to laugh or weep. It is the triumph of insignificance, the apotheosis of foppery and folly. It is the perfection of the mock-heroic!

Criticism in the nineteenth century continued very much on the lines set by Warton and then taken up by the Romantics. The Victorian Matthew Arnold pushed the Romantic attitude to a logical conclusion: 'though they may in a certain sense be masters of the art of versification, Dryden and Pope are not classics of our poetry, they are classics of our prose'. He went further: 'The difference between genuine poetry and the school of Dryden and Pope, and all their school, is briefly this; their poetry is conceived and composed in their wits, genuine poetry is conceived and composed in the soul.'

An indication that there was still a reading public for Pope in a period in which his poetry was not obviously fashionable are the illustrations of *The Rape of the Lock* by the chief artist of the aesthetic movement in the late nineteenth century, Aubrey Beardsley.

Upali Amarasinghe, *Dryden and Pope in the early Nineteenth Century*, Cambridge University Press, 1962

> A study of the complexities of the Romantic response to the Augustans

John Barnard, ed., *Pope: The Critical Heritage*, Routledge & Kegan Paul, 1973

> The critical reaction to Pope's poetry from 1705 to 1800. Contains a generous selection from Warton and Johnson, including all the quotations in this volume

W. Bateson & N.A. Joukovsky, eds, *Alexander Pope: A Critical Anthology*, Penguin Critical Anthologies, Harmondsworth, 1971

> Divided into three sections: I Contemporaneous Criticism and the Eighteenth Century: II The Continuing Debate: III Modern Views
>
> An excellent compendium, well indexed; contains Byron, Hazlitt and Arnold

V. Guerinot, *Pamphlet Attacks on Alexander Pope 1711–1744: A Descriptive Bibliography*, Methuen, 1969

> Evidence that Pope did not initiate attacks, that he was much provoked and that the literary world of the eighteenth century was far from polite

Robert Halsband, *The Rape of the Lock and Its Illustrations, 1714–1896*, Oxford University Press, 1980

> Visual evidence of the continuing popularity of the poem in the eighteenth and nineteenth centuries

THE TWENTIETH CENTURY

The **Romantic** and Arnoldian estimate of Pope has slowly been challenged in the twentieth century with the advent of modernism and a changed perspective on the nature of poetry. It is now more readily taken for granted that poetry can manifest itself in a variety of ways. Johnson's question (prompted doubtless by Warton's estimate) now seems unanswerable: 'If Pope is not a poet, where is poetry to be found?'

Practical criticism, a term associated with I.A. Richards (1893–1979), which required above all close and disciplined attention to the words on the page (in conscious reaction to more traditional literary historical approaches in which the text often was regarded as a piece of evidence for biographical or historical enquiry or the *belles-lettrist* approaches of the gifted amateur) has yielded fruitful studies of Pope's poetry. To these may be related revaluations inspired by F.R. Leavis (1895–1978), the founding editor of the influential journal *Scrutiny*, in the 1930s and the work of the self-styled **New Critics** of America in the 1930s and 1940s who treated the text as an autonomous entity to be investigated through close examination of its own interior dynamics. What these critics admired in poetry and felt gave it its strength and value, such things as the holding together of apparently contradictory views or impulses or the presence of **paradox, irony** and ambiguity, could be located in the poetry of Pope. These approaches had the effect of showing that his poetry was more complicated than had often been allowed in the nineteenth century.

Cleanth Brooks, 'The Case of Miss Arabella Fermor' in *The Well-Wrought Urn*, Harcourt Brace Javanovich Inc., 1947
> An American new critic

William Empson, *Seven Types of Ambiguity*, Chatto & Windus, 1930
> A pupil of I.A. Richards

F.R. Leavis, *Revaluation*, Chatto & Windus, 1936
> A landmark in modern criticism, revaluing seventeenth- and early eighteenth-century poetry, including Pope's, reversing the estimate of Arnold and late Romanticism

W.K. Wimsatt, 'Rhetoric and Poems' in *The Verbal Icon*, 1954
> An American new critic

HISTORICAL CRITICISM

Historical criticism has continued to flourish. A social poet whose work is so deeply embedded in the life of its times has been the legitimate subject of much contextual study. His biography, his social relations, his political affiliations have been the subject of minute scholarly attention in the belief that the satires, in particular, cannot be assessed without a firm sense of their topical context and a precise knowledge of their contemporary personal allusions. Satire is not a mode that is ideally suited to new critical procedures.

Howard Erskine Hill, *The Social Milieu of Alexander Pope: Lives, Example and the Poetic Response*, Yale University Press, 1975

> A detailed investigation of the many figures mentioned in Pope's poetry and of their social significance

Peter Dixon, *The World of Pope's Satires: An Introduction to the Epistles and Imitations of Horace*, Methuen, 1968

> An introduction to the *Epistles* and *Imitations of Horace*, elucidating their topicality and literary reference

Maynard Mack, *Alexander Pope: A Life*, Yale University Press, 1985

> A mine of information from a dedicated Popean

James M. Osborn, *Anecdotes, Observations and Character of Books and Men by Joseph Spence*, 2 vols., Oxford University Press, 1966

> Includes reports of Spence's own conversations with Pope

Pat Rogers, *Grub Street; Studies in a Sub-Culture*, Methuen, 1972

> Puts Pope's literary career in the context of the burgeoning publishing industry in the early eighteenth century and the rise of the popular press

Valerie Rumbold, *Women's Place in Pope's World*, Cambridge University Press, 1989

> A scholarly rather than a feminist account

George Sherburn, *The Early Career of Alexander Pope*, Princeton University Press, 1934

> Includes a useful account of early biographers

There is a category of Pope criticism that cannot be properly be labelled historical though it might be thought that it represents a subdivision of historical criticism, that addresses in a systematic way the nature of Pope's literary relations to previous poets. This principally concerns the two major affiliations in Pope's literary career with the Greek epic poet

Homer, whom he spent a decade translating, and the Roman poet Horace, a number of whose satires and epistles he updated in modern imitations in the last decade of his life.

Apart from the consideration of these two major literary relations, all his poetry is naturally allusive, echoing, sometimes ironically sometimes not, the literature of the past, particularly but not exclusively the poets of Greece and Rome. Allied to this is criticism that seeks to identify those inherited characteristics and generic traditions in the various literary kinds, such as verse satire, with which Pope is engaging, whether he is renewing, Englishing, adapting or subverting. Many such critics might argue that the tradition of genre is a key determining factor in all literary production but particularly in the case of a Neoclassical poet like Pope whose whole career can be said to be in dialogue with the classical tradition, from his early pastorals, modelled on those of the Roman Virgil, to his epic *Dunciad* ('Books and the man I sing' (1728)) which can be regarded as a parodic inversion of Virgil's epic poem the *Aeneid*, the opening words of which in Dryden's version (1697) are 'Arms and the man I sing'.

Reuben Brower, *The Poetry of Allusion*, Oxford University Press, 1959
> Relates Pope's poems in their various genres to their classical predecessors

A. Mason, *To Homer Through Pope*, Chatto & Windus, 1972
> A critical evaluation of Pope's Homer that examines its relation to the Greek, compares it with modern versions and raises the issues involved in creative translation

Frank Stack, *Pope and Horace*, Cambridge University Press, 1985
> A close study of the relation between the *Imitations of Horace* and their originals

Howard Weinbrot, *Alexander Pope and the Traditions of Formal Verse Satire*, Princeton University Press, 1982
> Relates the poetry to Horatian and Juvenalian satire

NEW THEORETICAL PERSPECTIVES

Most of what has been discussed so far may be called traditional in approach, at least when compared with some of the criticism of the last two decades, which has been influenced by the new wave of theoretical criticism, most of which started from France and spread quickly to the United States. The various strands of it cannot be very clearly differentiated in relation to what has been written on Pope but its general tendency may be indicated in what follows.

In *An Essay on Criticism*, Pope puts forward an ideal of critical practice which has at its heart an aspiration towards disinterestedness, the attempt to rise above prejudice, party spirit, idiosyncrasy, envy and above all pride and self-conceit in the common pursuit of true judgement. Underlying the *Essay* too is his core belief in the universal and unchanging light of nature, that is the 'source and end and test of art' (line 73). Involved in this is a belief that, whatever the differences of time and place, there is such a thing as an unchanging human essence, irrespective of cultural considerations. These are very much the views of the **Enlightenment** and in every respect they have been challenged by modern theorists, who deny the validity of a trans-historical human essence and assert that all human beings are the product of culturally formed and culturally mediated ideologies which preclude universality.

Ideology may be defined as the collection of ideas, opinions, values, beliefs and preoccupations that go to make up the 'mind-set' of a group of people, that is, the intellectual framework through which they view everything, and which colours all their attitudes and feelings (especially, perhaps, assumptions about power and authority). At root, this derives from Marx, for whom all literature is permeated by the ideology of the era and the class from which it is derived. No world-view is free from ideology. The task that many theorists set themselves is the unpicking or unmasking of Pope's hidden ideology.

On the back cover of a study of Pope cited below, the general editor summarises the approach as follows: 'Pope's poetry has, for the most part, been taken on its own terms. ... This book asks us to rethink such a way of understanding Pope. Refusing to accept Pope's version of reality, Laura Brown reads his poems not for what they claim to say, but for what they rationalise away or fail to recognise.' She argues that his poems are bound up with two interconnected issues: capitalism and imperialism. *The Rape of the Lock*, for example, is seen to relate to commodity fetishism resulting from recent mercantile expansion.

In all his poetry the universal values he advocates are, in fact, the values of his class, of a (would-be) patrician Tory under threat. Furthermore, his poetry betrays all the contradictions of a constructed ideology. His scorn for poverty-ridden hacks and dunces and his hatred of the popular forms of cultural expression conceal insecurities about his own rise from comparatively humble origins and about his dependence upon material benefits derived from his translation of Homer.

Laura Brown, *Alexander Pope*, Rereading Literature, Basil Blackwell, 1985

An account that seeks to expose the ideology hidden in the major poems

David Fairer, ed., *Pope: New Contexts*, Harvester Wheatsheaf, 1990

A series of essays by different contributors concerned with issues of gender and class

Brean Hammond, *Pope,* Harvester New Readings, The Harvester Press, 1986

A discussion of the most important poems in the light of modern theoretical perspectives

Current events	Author's life	Literary events
		1674 John Milton, poet, dies
		1684 John Gay, poet and dramatist, born; Pierre Corneille, creator of French classical tragedy, dies
1685 Charles II dies		
		1687 Edmund Waller, statesman and poet, dies
1688 James II flees to France; William of Orange and Mary accede to throne	**1688** Alexander Pope born, only son of a Catholic linen-merchant, Lombard St, London	
1689 Toleration Act allows freedom of worship for dissenters; Louis XIV declares war on England		
1690 Battle of the Boyne; William III defeats James II; East India Company founded	**1690s** Educated at home where he learns Greek and Latin, and at Catholic schools in Winchester and London; contracts TB	
		1697 John Dryden's *Aeneid*
		1699 Pierre Racine, French tragic dramatist dies
	1700 Goes to live with parents at Binfield, near Windsor Forest	**1700** Dryden dies
1701 Queen Anne succeeds William III; Act of Settlement; James II dies in France		
1702-13 War of Spanish Succession	**1702** Goes to London to learn French and Italian	
	1707 First meets Blount family	**1707** Farquhar, *The Beaux' Stratagem*
	1709 *Pastorals*	**1709** First issue of *The Tatler*
1710 Whig Ministry falls; Wren completes St Paul's Cathedral		

Current events	Author's life	Literary events
	1711 *An Essay on Criticism;* introduced to John Gay	**1711** Dennis, *On the Genius and Writings of Shakespeare*
	1712 First version of *The Rape of the Lock;* meets Addison	
	1713 *Windsor Forest;* meets Swift; attacks John Dennis; reproved by Addison; studies painting under Jervas	**1713** Addison, *Cato;* Gay, *Rural Sports* and *The Fan*
		1713-14 Meetings of Scriblerus Club, founded by Pope and Spence
1714 George I succeeds Queen Anne; non-members of Church of England forbidden to teach	**1714** Commissioned to translate *Iliad* (completed 1720); *Rape of the Lock* enlarged	
1715 First Jacobite uprising in Scotland; Walpole made Chancellor of Exchequer	**1715-16** Quarrels with Addison	
	1716 Settles with parents in Chiswick, London	**1716** Lady Mary Wortley Montagu, *Town Eclogues* and *Court Poems,* piratically published by Curll
1717 Walpole resigns; Handel's 'Water Music'	**1717** *Eloisa to Abelard; Works;* first quarrels with Colley Cibber; father dies	**1717** *Three Hours After Marriage,* play by Gay, Pope and Arbuthnot; Daniel Defoe, *Robinson Crusoe;* Voltaire imprisoned for his satires in La Bastille
	1718 Moves to Twickenham with mother	**1718** Thomas Parnell, poet and friend of Pope dies; Lady Mary Wortley Montagu returns to England from Constantinople
1719-20 The painter Watteau in London to seek treatment for TB		**1719** Joseph Addison dies
1720 South Sea Bubble bursts		
1721 Walpole becomes first Lord of Treasury and first Prime Minister		

Y

World events	Author's life	Literary events
	1725 His edition of *Shakespeare,* attacked by Theobald; Swift pays long visit to him	
	1725-6 His translation of *Odyssey*	
		1726-9 Voltaire exiled in England
1727 George II succeeds George I		
1728 Queen's Square, Bath, begun in Palladian style; Bach's *St Matthew's Passion*	**1728** *The Dunciad* (Books I-III)	**1728** Gay, *Beggar's Opera*
1730 Wesleys start Methodist Society	**1730** Quarrels with Aaron Hill and others	**1730** Colley Cibber made Poet Laureate; founding of *Grub-street Journal*
		1732 Voltaire, *Zaïre,* heroic tragedy
	1733 Mother dies, aged 93; quarrels with Lord Hervey	
	1733-8 *Imitations of Horace*	
	1734 *An Essay on Man*	**1734** Gay dies
1735 Hogarth, *A Rake's Progress*	**1735** *Epistle to Dr Arbuthnot*	**1735** Dr John Arbuthnot dies
1738 Freemasonry attacked in papal bull	**1738** *Epilogue to Satires*	
		1739 Lady Mary Wortley Montagu leaves England
1740 War of Austrian succession begins	**1740** Close of correspondence with Swift	
		1742 Henry Fielding, *Joseph Andrews*
	1743 Revisions to *Dunciad*	
	1744 Dies at Twickenham, surrounded by friends	
1745 Jacobite Rebellion		**1745** Swift dies

allegory a story or situation described in such a way as to have two coherent meanings

anaphora (Greek, 'carrying back, repetition') the name for a rhetorical device, in which a word or phrase is repeated in several successive clauses. Often this kind of syntactical device is associated with the depiction of strong feelings: 'Not youthful kings in battle seized alive, / Not scornful virgins who their charm survives'

antithesis (from the Greek meaning 'opposite placing') a rhetorical term describing the opposition of contrasting ideas in neighbouring sentences or clauses, using opposite forms of words: 'Willing to wound, yet afraid to strike'

apostrophe (Greek, 'turning away') a rhetorical term for speech addressed to a person, idea, or thing, often deliberately interrupting the narrative flow for dramatic effect: 'O thoughtless mortals, ever blind to fate'

Augustan derived from the name of Rome's first emperor who ruled from 27BC to AD14, a time of peace and prosperity in which the leading poets Virgil and Horace were patronised by the regime to which they gave their support; sometimes used to denote qualities of urbanity, poise, refinement and restraint embodied in the Roman poets and aspired to by English poets

blank verse unrhymed iambic pentameter

chiasmus (Greek, 'crossing over') a common figure of speech in which the word order of similar phrases is inverted: 'A fop their passion, but their prize a sot'

correctness artistic polish and refinement

end-stopped the end of a line coincides with an essential grammatical pause

enjambement a line of poetry which is not end-stopped, and the sentence naturally runs over to the next line without a pause

Enlightenment a term for aspects of the intellectual atmosphere of Europe, especially in France, during the eighteenth century. The overriding feature of this phase of thought was the conviction that reason would solve the problems of humanity and rid the world of all undesirable elements, superstition, barbarity and ignorance. Reason was thought to lead naturally to scientific discovery

epithet an adjective or adjectival phrase which defines a special quality or attribute, like 'the finny tribe' for 'fish'

figurative language, figures of speech (Latin, to shape, form or conceive) any form of expression or grammar which deviates from the plainest expression of meaning is designated a 'figure of speech'. These may be figures which alter the sense (tropes), like metaphor, or figures of arrangement, like antithesis which by their patterning give emphasis and memorability

genre a distinct kind of literature, such as pastoral, mock epic, verse epistle or detective fiction with its own conventions and characteristics. These are never fixed; if they were, change and development would be impossible, but they may have great influence upon works of art as practitioners renew, adapt or subvert them

Gothic literature or architecture of an obsessive, gloomy and spine-chilling atmosphere, in imitation of the medieval

heroic couplet lines of iambic pentameter rhymed in pairs. In Neoclassical verse they tend to be closed; the syntax coincides with the metre so that each pair of lines is a sentence

Historical criticism a system that assesses literature within its historical perspective

humanist a scholar of the 'humanities', that is classical literature; reason, balance and a proper dignity for man were the central ideals of humanist thought based upon the Renaissance revival of ancient ideals of human life and living

hyperbole (Greek, 'throwing too far') a figure of speech that emphasises by exaggeration; 'Then flashed the living lightning from her eyes'

iambic pentameter a line of five iambic feet – an iamb being a weak stress followed by a strong stress (e.g. ti-tum)

ideology (Greek, 'a discourse about or study of ideas') the collection of ideas, opinions, values, beliefs and preoccupations which go to make up a 'mind-set' of a group of people, that is, the intellectual framework through which they view everything, and which colours all their attitudes and feelings (especially, perhaps, assumptions about power and authority). What we take to be 'reality' is controlled by the ideologies of the era in which we live

imitation a work in which a writer consciously updates the work of a previous writer with contemporary language and topical allusions irony saying one thing while meaning another

masculine rhyme a monosyllabic rhyme on the final stressed syllables of two lines of verse, as contrasted with feminine rhyme, rhymed words of two or more syllables when the last syllable is not stressed (e.g. ladle / cradle)

metaphor (Greek, 'carrying over') a metaphor goes further than a comparison between two different things or ideas by fusing them together; one thing is described as being another thing, thus 'carrying over' all its associations

mock heroic refers to the style of mock epic where a trivial subject is treated with ridiculous comic grandeur

moral essay the name given by an early editor of Pope to his particular blend of satire and praise in his verse epistles

Neoclassical (Greek 'new' and Latin 'classic') an adjective denoting any literature and art in the Renaissance, seventeenth or eighteenth century that sought to conform to the rules or models of Greek or Latin antiquity. The literature of the period from 1660 to 1750 is particularly marked by this tendency

New criticism a movement in the 1930s and 1940s which studied a piece of literature as autonomous, rather than as a piece of biographical or sociological evidence or literary-historical material

oxymoron (Greek, 'pointedly foolish') a witty paradoxical expression, often containing a conjunction of opposites: 'bitter sweet'

panegyric a speech or poem wholeheartedly praising someone

paradox (Greek, 'contrary to popular opinion or expectation') a seemingly self-contradictory statement, which is yet shown in a surprising way to be true: 'There drinking largely sobers us again'

parody an imitation of a work of literature designed to ridicule its characteristic feature

periphrasis an indirect manner of describing or speaking: circumlocution

Practical criticism a style of criticism endorsed by Leavis, in which literature was examined and analysed, working from the particular towards an understanding of writers and periods rhetoric (Greek, 'art of speaking') the art of speaking and writing effectively so as to persuade an audience

Romantic a period term used for the literature and art produced in the wake of the French revolution of 1789 until roughly 1830; the literature of this period consciously turned its back on the ideals and practices of Neoclassical poets. The term is often contrasted with the classic or the Neoclassic

rules guidelines derived from observation of the best practice of the ancient writers covering all aspects of composition, often associated with the name of Aristotle for his *Poetics* (*c*.340BC) which had described the principles on which the best sort of tragedy worked

satire literature which exhibits or examines vice and folly and makes them appear ridiculous

sense a charged word in the eighteenth century, suggesting a special kind of intellectual stolidity and balanced intelligence

simile a comparison or likeness

wit (Old English, 'to know') originally meaning 'sense', 'understanding' or 'intelligence' it came to be used for the poetic intelligence including the imaginative faculty and might equally well apply to the author as to the work produced

zeugma (Greek, 'yoking') a figure of speech In which words or phrases with widely different meanings are 'yoked together' with comic effect by being made syntactically dependent on the same word, often a verb, as in 'counsel take or tea'

Author of this note

Robin Sowerby studied Classics and English at Cambridge. He now lectures in the Department of English Studies at Stirling University. He has written York Notes on Homer's *Iliad* and *Odyssey*, Virgil's *Aeneid*, Plato's *Republic* and York Advanced Notes on Shakespeare's *Antony and Cleopatra* and *As You Like It*. He has edited selections from Dryden and Pope, and is the author of *The Classical Legacy in Renaissance Poetry*, Longman, 1994.

York Notes Advanced

Margaret Atwood
Cat's Eye

Margaret Atwood
The Handmaid's Tale

Jane Austen
Mansfield Park

Jane Austen
Persuasion

Jane Austen
Pride and Prejudice

Alan Bennett
Talking Heads

William Blake
Songs of Innocence and of Experience

Charlotte Brontë
Jane Eyre

Emily Brontë
Wuthering Heights

Angela Carter
Nights at the Circus

Geoffrey Chaucer
The Franklin's Prologue and Tale

Geoffrey Chaucer
The Miller's Prologue and Tale

Geoffrey Chaucer
Prologue To the Canterbury Tales

Geoffrey Chaucer
The Wife of Bath's Prologue and Tale

Samuel Taylor Coleridge
Selected Poems

Joseph Conrad
Heart of Darkness

Daniel Defoe
Moll Flanders

Charles Dickens
Great Expectations

Charles Dickens
Hard Times

Emily Dickinson
Selected Poems

John Donne
Selected Poems

Carol Ann Duffy
Selected Poems

George Eliot
Middlemarch

George Eliot
The Mill on the Floss

T.S. Eliot
Selected Poems

F. Scott Fitzgerald
The Great Gatsby

E.M. Forster
A Passage to India

Brian Friel
Translations

Thomas Hardy
The Mayor of Casterbridge

Thomas Hardy
The Return of the Native

Thomas Hardy
Selected Poems

Thomas Hardy
Tess of the d'Urbervilles

Seamus Heaney
Selected Poems from Opened Ground

Nathaniel Hawthorne
The Scarlet Letter

Kazuo Ishiguro
The Remains of the Day

Ben Jonson
The Alchemist

James Joyce
Dubliners

John Keats
Selected Poems

Christopher Marlowe
Doctor Faustus

Arthur Miller
Death of a Salesman

John Milton
Paradise Lost Books I & II

Toni Morrison
Beloved

Alexander Pope
Rape of the Lock and other poems

William Shakespeare
Antony and Cleopatra

William Shakespeare
As You Like It

William Shakespeare
Hamlet

William Shakespeare
King Lear

William Shakespeare
Measure for Measure

William Shakespeare
The Merchant of Venice

William Shakespeare
A Midsummer Night's Dream

William Shakespeare
Much Ado About Nothing

William Shakespeare
Othello

William Shakespeare
Richard II

William Shakespeare
Romeo and Juliet

William Shakespeare
The Taming of the Shrew

William Shakespeare
The Tempest

William Shakespeare
The Winter's Tale

George Bernard Shaw
Saint Joan

Mary Shelley
Frankenstein

Alice Walker
The Color Purple

Oscar Wilde
The Importance of Being Earnest

Tennessee Williams
A Streetcar Named Desire

John Webster
The Duchess of Malfi

Virginia Woolf
To the Lighthouse

W.B. Yeats
Selected Poems

Chinua Achebe
Things Fall Apart

Jane Austen
Emma

Jane Austen
Northanger Abbey

Jane Austen
Sense and Sensibility

Samuel Beckett
Waiting for Godot and
Endgame

Louis de Bernières
Captain Corelli's Mandolin

Charlotte Brontë
Villette

Geoffrey Chaucer
The Merchant's Tale

Geoffrey Chaucer
The Nun's Priest's Tale

Caryl Churchill
Top Girls and *Cloud Nine*

Charles Dickens
Bleak House

T.S. Eliot
The Waste Land

Henry Fielding
Joseph Andrews

Anne Frank
The Diary of Anne Frank

Thomas Hardy
Jude the Obscure

Homer
The Iliad

Homer
The Odyssey

Henrik Ibsen
The Doll's House and *Ghosts*

Ben Jonson
Volpone

James Joyce
*A Portrait of the Artist as a
Young Man*

Philip Larkin
Selected Poems

Aldous Huxley
Brave New World

D.H. Lawrence
Selected Poems

Christopher Marlowe
Edward II

John Milton
Paradise Lost Bks IV & IX

Thomas More
Utopia

George Orwell
Nineteen Eighty-four

Sylvia Plath
Selected Poems

J.B. Priestley
When We Are Married

Jean Rhys
Wide Sargasso Sea

William Shakespeare
As You Like It

William Shakespeare
Coriolanus

William Shakespeare
Henry IV Pt I

Wliiam Shakespeare
Henry IV Part II

William Shakespeare
Henry V

William Shakespeare
Julius Caesar

William Shakespeare
Macbeth

William Shakespeare
Richard III

William Shakespeare
Sonnets

William Shakespeare
Twelfth Night

Tom Stoppard
Arcadia and *Rosencrantz and
Guildenstern are Dead*

Jonathan Swift
*Gulliver's Travels and A Modest
Proposal*

Alfred, Lord Tennyson
Selected Poems

Virgil
The Aeneid

Edith Wharton
Ethan Frome

Jeanette Winterson
*Oranges are Not the Only
Fruit*

Tennessee Williams
Cat on a Hot Tin Roof

Virginia Woolf
Mrs Dalloway

Metaphysical Poets

GCSE and equivalent levels

Maya Angelou
I Know Why the Caged Bird Sings

Jane Austen
Pride and Prejudice

Alan Ayckbourn
Absent Friends

Elizabeth Barrett Browning
Selected Poems

Robert Bolt
A Man for All Seasons

Harold Brighouse
Hobson's Choice

Charlotte Brontë
Jane Eyre

Emily Brontë
Wuthering Heights

Shelagh Delaney
A Taste of Honey

Charles Dickens
David Copperfield

Charles Dickens
Great Expectations

Charles Dickens
Hard Times

Charles Dickens
Oliver Twist

Roddy Doyle
Paddy Clarke Ha Ha Ha

George Eliot
Silas Marner

George Eliot
The Mill on the Floss

William Golding
Lord of the Flies

Oliver Goldsmith
She Stoops To Conquer

Willis Hall
The Long and the Short and the Tall

Thomas Hardy
Far from the Madding Crowd

Thomas Hardy
The Mayor of Casterbridge

Thomas Hardy
Tess of the d'Urbervilles

Thomas Hardy
The Withered Arm and other Wessex Tales

L.P. Hartley
The Go-Between

Seamus Heaney
Selected Poems

Susan Hill
I'm the King of the Castle

Barry Hines
A Kestrel for a Knave

Louise Lawrence
Children of the Dust

Harper Lee
To Kill a Mockingbird

Laurie Lee
Cider with Rosie

Arthur Miller
The Crucible

Arthur Miller
A View from the Bridge

Robert O'Brien
Z for Zachariah

Frank O'Connor
My Oedipus Complex and Other Stories

George Orwell
Animal Farm

J.B. Priestley
An Inspector Calls

Willy Russell
Educating Rita

Willy Russell
Our Day Out

J.D. Salinger
The Catcher in the Rye

William Shakespeare
Henry IV Part 1

William Shakespeare
Henry V

William Shakespeare
Julius Caesar

William Shakespeare
Macbeth

William Shakespeare
The Merchant of Venice

William Shakespeare
A Midsummer Night's Dream

William Shakespeare
Much Ado About Nothing

William Shakespeare
Romeo and Juliet

William Shakespeare
The Tempest

William Shakespeare
Twelfth Night

George Bernard Shaw
Pygmalion

Mary Shelley
Frankenstein

R.C. Sherriff
Journey's End

Rukshana Smith
Salt on the Snow

John Steinbeck
Of Mice and Men

Robert Louis Stevenson
Dr Jekyll and Mr Hyde

Jonathan Swift
Gulliver's Travels

Robert Swindells
Daz 4 Zoe

Mildred D. Taylor
Roll of Thunder, Hear My Cry

Mark Twain
Huckleberry Finn

James Watson
Talking in Whispers

William Wordsworth
Selected Poems

A Choice of Poets

Mystery Stories of the Nineteenth Century including The Signalman

Nineteenth Century Short Stories

Poetry of the First World War

Six Women Poets

NOTES